LIGHTNING
SALES OPS

LIGHTNING SALES OPS

**Building Salesforce for
Sales Development Teams**

MATT BERTUZZI

I am a Salesforce MVP. For more information on the Salesforce MVP community, visit: http://www.salesforce.com/mvp/. Salesforce, success.salesforce.com, Chatter, Data.com, and others are trademarks of salesforce.com, inc. and are used here with permission. All other trademarks are the property of their respective owners.

LIBRARY OF CONGRESS CATALOGING-IN-PUBLICATION DATA
Bertuzzi, Matt. Lightning Sales Ops: building Salesforce for sales development teams / by Matt Bertuzzi.

First Edition
ISBN 978-0-692-84405-2

10 9 8 7 6 5 4 3 2 1

for Kira, who made me take out the puns.

CONTENTS

INTRODUCTION

⚡

IF YOU WERE TO head over to www.google.com and type in the incomplete phrase *why is salesforce so,* you'd likely find some interesting auto-complete suggestions. For me right now, they include "good," "slow," "successful," and "ugly."

A visitor from another world—who knew nothing more about Salesforce than what they learned from Google—would have quite a contradictory picture of the platform.

But the more I think about it, these opposing streams provide a reasonably accurate picture of the state of Salesforce for most sales teams. Traditionally, customer relationship management (CRM) has been aimed at managers—and built on the backs of users. Since you're reading these words, I'll assume your company has or is considering a sales development team.

Let me ask you, do your sales development representatives (SDRs) often remark about how much they love using Salesforce? Do they feel bad for peers at other companies with poorly configured CRMs? Are they thankful that, unlike those poor sods, they aren't drowning in manual steps and byzantine processes.

I suspect this isn't a sentiment you hear very often.

I've asked dozens of SDRs to describe the experience of *doing their jobs inside Salesforce.* The responses ranged from "death by a thousand cuts" to "running in mud wearing cement shoes" to "sitting in the dentist's chair five days a week." I once heard "it's fine" and considered that rather high praise indeed.

Before we get too far, here's what I mean by sales development:

*A specialized role focused on the frontend of the sales process—
qualifying inbound leads and/or conducting outbound
prospecting. Titles include ADRs, BDRs, LGRs, MDRs, or similar.*

In recent years, sales development has emerged as a critical discipline and lever for revenue growth. It has been billed as "the hottest job in sales," "the most important sales process innovation in 10 years," and earned its own technology stack.

Since 2012, more than a dozen companies have built tools for "activity management," "personalized outbound," and "inside sales acceleration." North of $300M in venture funding has poured into this space. The category is white-hot and many of those tools are fantastic. This movement is, in part, an attempt to simplify, streamline, and automate the parts of the job made tedious by traditional CRM.

My goal, and the focus of this book, is to maximize the investment you've already made. Rather than fleeing Salesforce to do their work, I want Salesforce to go to work *for* your reps. Together, we'll take your reps from the "dentist's chair" to the cockpit of a finely-tuned productivity machine. Making Salesforce sleek, streamlining processes, and boosting productivity will be our aims.

Whether you're an SDR leader or in sales operations. Whether your business card reads business analyst or salesforce admin. I'm sure you'll agree that your company's growth depends on how effectively you acquire new pipeline. Sales development done well leads to a wave of new prospects entering the pipeline and a steady stream of new logos becoming customers. It's no wonder the role receives so much investment and attention.

But let me ask you another question. Does your company think of the SDRs themselves as internal customers? Have you spent much time considering their user experience inside Salesforce? I'm not referring to the outputs they're (often tediously) measured on. But to the actual user experience they encounter day after day, dial after dial, prospect after prospect, click after click.

If you haven't, you aren't alone.

I wrote this book for three reasons. One, for all the attention and buzz the SDR role has received, the way companies *support sales development in Salesforce* hasn't advanced much in the last 10 years. Where account executives, managers, and senior leaders have been drowning in innovation and improvement, SDRs have been logging clicks and filling fields in ways that would be entirely familiar to a time traveler from 2008. In case you weren't in the workforce in 2008, yes Salesforce was around back then.

The second reason is that Salesforce has (finally!) given us the tools to enable rather than encumber our SDRs. In August 2015, the Salesforce Lightning Experience debuted. In a blog post entitled *Welcome to the Future of CRM. Welcome to Salesforce Lightning*, Salesforce boasted:

> *"A completely new CRM experience that is going to accelerate adoption and value for every Salesforce customer and end user. This launch is not just about new fonts and colors and icons. And it's about much more than a refreshed user interface. Lightning Experience is a completely new Salesforce and a completely new way to sell."*

Like any sales operation/Salesforce admin worth my salt, I rolled my eyes. But in the year and a half since I first "met" Lightning, I've found it to be the single biggest opportunity for improving user experience and accelerating the front-end of the sales process.

If you aren't familiar with the Lightning Experience, don't worry. You needn't be a "LEX-pert" (groan) to get value from this book. In fact, you don't even need to be a Salesforce guru. But you do have to have a sales operations mindset. That means a commitment to improving user experience and a passion for designing subtle yet powerful automation.

The final reason I wrote this book is you. Yes, you! Far too often, sales operations professionals judge success by the absence of nasty emails and not the presence of praise. There are more requests, complaints, and changes of direction in a single quarter than anyone can reasonably be expected to handle. But at our best, sales operations pros are the "utility infielders" and "chiefs of staff" for senior sales leaders and chief revenue officers. I recently saw a job post for a *Head of Sales Operations, Global Sales Development* and this line caught my eye:

> *"For individuals who aspire to eventually operate as a general manager or CEO, this role is an opportunity to learn the key skills of running a global sales organization."*

If you have those aspirations, it is my most sincere hope that this book supports you and helps to propel your career forward.

This book is organized into five parts: *Identify, Plan, Contact, Qualify,* and *Report.* Rather than follow an object-oriented approach, I've taken the point of view of SDRs working in Salesforce. We'll begin with identifying prospects, followed by conducting pre-call planning, then initiating contact and so on. These five parts are the byproduct of twelve years in sales, eight years on the Salesforce platform, and a whole lot of trial and error—taking note of mistakes and building upon success. I often joke that I'm a *recovering sales guy* as I've been both an SDR and an account executive. Today, I'm a Salesforce user group leader, a five-time Dreamforce presenter, and a Salesforce MVP. But in my heart, I'll always be sales operations and a button-click Salesforce admin.

Some of the ideas in this book you may have already put into practice. A few you might even disagree with. That's good. The beauty of the Salesforce platform is the ability to design parallel solutions to reach the same need. But if you truly want to nail sales operations for sales development, the sum of all five parts is greater than the whole.

I interviewed 34 sales executives, SDR leaders, marketers, operations pros, and Salesforce admins for this book. I hope the stories, strategies, and thinking I share will inspire you. Each chapter contains both lecture and lab. First, I'll share the *why* and *what* of each concept—the lecture. Then I'll present the *how* of building it in Salesforce—the lab. If you're a sales leader, SDR manager, or non-Salesforce admin, you can skim the technical bits. If you're an admin, I'd encourage you to dig into the whys and whats as well as the hows. As the title of one of my favorite Dreamforce sessions declares, *being a Salesforce admin means being a business analyst.* And that means getting at why business users are asking for changes before diving into what they're asking for.

I couldn't be any more thrilled that you've decided to take this journey with me. Let's get started.

PART 1

IDENTIFY

Humans are allergic to change. They love to say, "We've always done it this way." I try to fight that. That's why I have a clock on my wall that runs counter-clockwise.

—REAR ADMIRAL DR. GRACE HOPPER

CHAPTER 1

⚡

SUPPORT YOUR SDRS IN SALESFORCE

IN NOVEMBER 2009, I gave a talk at a local user group meeting on tricks for making Salesforce work for Sales Development Reps (SDRs). We called them *tricks* back then as the era of labelling everything a "hack" had yet to be born. The burning insights I highlighted were to 1) create a picklist where reps can select a prospect's time zone on a lead record and 2) to create a new field to store direct dial phone numbers. It went over really well. Believe it or not, in a room full of 20+ tech companies with sales development teams, no one had made either customization.

That talk was the genesis of this book.

It helped me to see that managers want to make life simpler for their SDRs, but they lack the tools, tips, and *hacks* to do so. A few years later, I attended a sales development event at OpenView, a Massachusetts expansion-stage venture capital firm. The attendees talked about a day in the life of an SDR and the headwinds they face inside their CRM implementations. Again, simple tweaks and reporting tips were greeted with nodding heads and great Q&A.

Then at Dreamforce 2015, Salesforce MVP Rebecca Dente and I presented on making sales development hum with advanced automation. We got nerdy and talked about formula fields, Process Builder, and Visual Workflow; all roads leading to enabling SDR success with clever customization and process automation.

The through line for all those talks was this: *sales development reps are your highest volume Salesforce users*. Yet in terms of support, they get the

7

scraps. These reps have a tough job. They reach out to generally unsuspecting (and often unwilling) prospects to set meetings for their account executive counterparts. Whether they're qualifying inbound interest or outbound prospecting to generate opportunity, there they are working away inside Salesforce. All day, every day. But most Salesforce instances haven't been built to make their lives any easier. In fact, most of the instances I've logged into offer resistance, not acceleration. And in some, CRM might as well stand for *crazy, riddled mess.*

For these high volume, high output, and high impact teams, the SDR strategy has too often been *more.* More manual processes, more clicks, more required fields, and ultimately more aggravation.

It isn't just sales leaders and the C-suite that deserve the blame. I've been critical of Salesforce over the years for overlooking this group of users. At Dreamforce '13 when Salesforce1 was launched, I wondered "what about the non-road warriors?". When it was proclaimed that anyone could run their business from their phone I snarked, "there's a word for people who can do their job from a tablet and it is overhead." For the heads in headsets crowd, and those that manage or support them, there was little to feast on but thin gruel.

This *SDRs eat last* mindset is totally backwards. SDRs may be your company's most valuable employees. Ilya Semin is CEO of sales intelligence and technographics company Datanyze. "I believe that sales development representatives are integral to the success of any B2B company," he published on LinkedIn. "Think about how much time and money you spend on marketing and PR campaigns hoping to create a specific image and reputation for your brand. Yet in reality, sales development reps personify your company. They must walk the walk of all that marketing copy."

A Hierarchy of Sales Force Automation

Ask any SDR or account executive, "who is Salesforce built for?" And you'll get a nearly identical reply: *management.* I've tried to take a different tack in this book. I've attempted to focus on serving the sales development reps themselves. Yes, you'll find a lot that will fuel reporting for sales managers and senior executives. But my hierarchy of thinking is shown in figure 1.1 below:

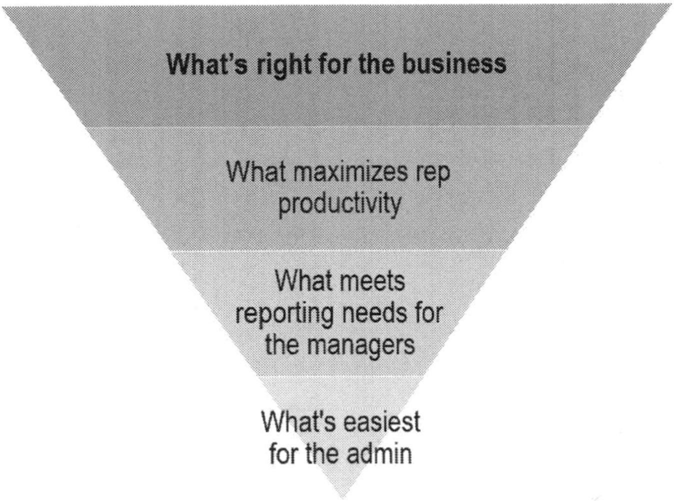

What's right for the business

What maximizes rep
productivity

What meets
reporting needs for
the managers

What's easiest
for the admin

Figure 1.1 – Hierarchy of sales enablement

To my fellow admins, I'm sorry to say that the heavy lifting falls to us. To guide you, I've held to three principles in this book.

1. **Clicks, not code**
    Everything we're going to be building is 100% declarative (meaning no code required). You don't need to be a developer to implement anything you'll read in this book. Also, I've focused on native solutions, not third party tools. I know how hard it can be to fight for budget and I want to support you getting the most out of the Salesforce platform.

2. **Lightning-first**
    Perhaps you haven't moved your SDRs to Lightning yet. I understand, migrating can feel daunting. By the end of this book, I expect you'll see why I'm so bullish on the Lightning Experience. This isn't just a reskin and a rebrand, it is a reimagining of what is possible within Salesforce.

3. No overly creative solutions

In architecting solutions, it's easy to lose the plot. I tried to take a minimally viable approach—solving the core need and leaving you with room to expand and customize for your business. I often reminded myself of this tweet from Steven Herod, principal director at Accenture (figure 1.2). That's a Lord of the Rings reference in case you aren't fully versed in the sacred texts of the nerds.

When someone suggests an overly creative technical solution:

The Dwarves delved too greedily and too deep

The Dwarves delved too greedily and too deep
youtube.com

Figure 1.2 – Tweet from @sherod

This book is divided into five parts. Each focuses on a specific portion of the SDR workflow. Part 1: Identify - Focuses on getting the right prospect to the right SDR at the right time.

Part 2: Plan - Presents stories and approaches for shortening the distance between valuable context and your reps' fingertips. We'll go deep on building pre-call planning into Salesforce.

In Part 3: Contact - Offers a roadmap for making Salesforce workable for SDRs. These chapters are filled with actionable advice for tracking outreach, implementing a cadence process, and measuring results.

Part 4: Qualify – This section is all about the passing meetings from SDR to account executive. Handoff, qualification criteria, and acceptance process are discussed in great detail.

Part 5: Measure - Switches gears and present strategies and examples for measuring sales development impact. There's a lot to learn about dashboard for executive management, marketing, first-line managers, and the reps themselves. So those topics are covered in depth.

Salesforce practically has a language all its own. *Salesfortuguese?* Throughout this book, I've used a formatting system to make things more clear. I've referred to objects in *italics,* field names in **Bold**, and field values in "quotation marks." For example, Sally set the **Lead Source** on *Leads* to "Website." Whenever a button is mentioned I've placed it in [brackets]. Sort of looks like a button, no? Thanks to my father-in-law Tom for that suggestion!

Over the *strong* objections of my good friend Rebecca Dente, I decided to print this book in black and white. I must admit the figures are truly breathtaking in full color. You can access a color PDF of all the figures presented in this book by visiting http://sdrbook.io/lightningops (all lowercase).

Okay, let's get started.

CHAPTER 2

⚡

THINK LIKE AN ENGINEER

IMAGINE FOR A MOMENT, that you are an inbound SDR. You're given a prospect who has taken action in response to a marketing activity (e.g., filled out a web form, signed-up for a trial, attended a webinar, etc.). Your job is to reach out, qualify them, and book a meeting for one of your account executive counterparts. Obviously, there are many variations of this model, but let's keep things simple for now.

Before you pick up the phone, you might run through a pre-flight checklist similar to figure 2.1 below:

Is this lead from a current customer?	Y / N
Is this lead from an account with an active opportunity?	Y / N
Has an AE worked this account recently?	Y / N
Is another SDR working a different prospect(s) at this account?	Y / N
Is another SDR working a dupe of this prospect?	Y / N
Okay, this is my lead.	
Are they a real person?	Y / N
Is this company a good fit?	Y / N
Is there anything interesting in their campaign history / website activities?	Y / N
Are there nuggets I can uncover in pre-call research on this prospect or their company?	Y / N

Do I have a good theme or reason for making this call?	Y / N
Do I know what time zone they are in?	Y / N
Can I find a direct dial phone number?	Y / N
Okay, I'm ready to make this call.	

Figure 2.1 – SDR checklist

In this simplified example that's twelve different questions that need to be answered before you'd be ready to make a minimally effective first call. Now, what does that process look like in Salesforce?

1. You pop over to your "Hot Leads" list view and see your new prospect. You click into the record and copy the person's name. In another tab, you search *Contacts* and *Accounts* to make sure the contact isn't being worked by another rep. Then you flip over to an open LinkedIn tab and search for the person. You find they weren't 100% honest with their title, so you update their information and save the record.

2. Next, you open up another tab to Google the company. You find a few pre-call research nuggets that you'd like to reference later. You jump back to the record in Salesforce and add some notes to a text field.

3. Next, you confirm what their recent campaign activity involved. Perhaps it's a recent webinar, so you head over to your email to find the email from marketing with all the details. So far, you have five open tabs and more than ten clicks back and forth. You haven't even made your first call yet.

4. Next, you change the **Lead Status** from "Open-MQL" to "Working" and dial their number. They don't answer, you leave a voicemail, and log the call.

I asked ten SDRs from different companies to show me how they execute that exact process in Salesforce. Guess how many clicks it took them? On average, *fourteen*. And that's just for the first voicemail. What happens next? Emma Lehman is a former SDR, a former SDR manager, and present-day

13

Director of Customer Success at QuotaFactory. We discussed the different steps and actions an SDR has to take after having just one conversation. "Say they connect with a prospect. There are all these little things they have to do after they hang up. They have to log the call, enter their notes, and if they learned any qualification information, fill in those fields. Usually they have to schedule a follow-up task," she shared. "If they spoke to the right person, they have to change the status for all leads at that company. They have to create the meeting as an event or opportunity and assign it to the correct AE. They have to prepare the agenda for the meeting and send out a calendar invite. I white boarded it all out once. I came up with fifty-two potential fields to update, records to create, and follow-ups to schedule."

Fifty-two!

On top of all that, reps are racing the clock. A mountain of research has focused on the importance of lead response time. In InsideSales.com's *Lead Response Management Study*, researchers found:

▶ Reps are ten times more likely to "contact" a lead if they call within the first hour of the prospect submitting a form.

▶ Reps are six times more likely to "qualify" a lead if they call within the first hour.

That's pretty convincing.

But how can any SDR be expected to meet those response times if every call takes fourteen clicks? And after every conversation, there are up to fifty-two actions to complete? Imagine that process, dial after dial repeated nine hundred or so times a month. *Shudder*. This leaves you with two choices. One, change the laws of space and time to give reps a chance at meeting speed-to-first-attempt goals. Or, two, remove the friction from Salesforce.

Sales development has a simple formula:

RESULTS = (Quantity of Effort x Quality of Effort) - Friction

We in sales operations can support our SDR teams to boost the quantity of their effort. Adding new tools to the technology stack is one way to accomplish this. We can even help to boost the quality of effort, by making key information and insight easier to access. But the single biggest lever we can pull is reducing the amount of friction in the process.

Sales operations isn't just about making your organization better at bean counting. We are, at our core, friction-reduction engineers and productivity artists. It can get too easy, in the daily hustle and bustle, to take on a triage mentality—"today, I have to knock down what's in front of me. I'll think bigger picture when I can catch my breath."

There's a line from author and management thinker Gary Hamel that I often come back to: *think like an engineer and feel like an artist.* As you make your way through this book, I hope you'll be inspired to do just that.

CHAPTER 3

⚡

TO LEAD OR NOT TO LEAD

IN THE BEGINNING, there were leads. No, seriously. As far back as I can remember, the "leads" tab has been an accepted part of prospecting in Salesforce. Salesforce Help & Training offers us this:

> *Track prospects apart from your contacts and opportunities with Salesforce lead records. After you've qualified your lead records, convert them to contacts and create accounts for them (if you don't already have the accounts in Salesforce). And hopefully, create opportunities to bolster your pipeline.*

By design, prospects start as a *Lead*, are promoted to a *Contact* and *Account*, and if we're lucky they turn into an *Opportunity*. This is how we operate because this is how Salesforce (the product) operates.

But not everyone agrees.

Cathy Otocka is founder and partner at MTI Solutions & Consulting. But to me, she'll always be my Martin Luther. (You know, the German one with his *95 Theses*.) Cathy has the honor of being the first person to challenge an orthodoxy so central to Salesforce that it borders on heresy. Namely, saying no to *Leads*. "People get stuck, emotionally, on the fact that Salesforce built a separate leads database. And that somehow, this implied a necessary part of the architecture. There are so many apps and so much custom code trying to deal with the fact that leads are apart from the rest of the database."

"People have a strong attachment to the gray lead convert button on leads. They get stuck in the belief that it's the only mechanism available to indicate business significance," Cathy shared. "My 'no leads' policy is really just a policy of 100% lead conversion. If a human is going to take action on a prospect, it shouldn't happen within the leads database."

Cathy makes a compelling case. She isn't advocating that we dump *Leads* entirely. But rather that if an SDR is going to interact with a record that they do so in the full context of the other side of the database (*Contacts, Accounts, Opportunities*, etc.). Yes, web-to-lead and marketing automation should integrate with *Leads*. But the real question is where should your SDRs be working day in and day out?

Let's return to our inbound inquiry from the previous chapter. Reviewing the first five questions on our checklist gives us:

Is this lead from a current customer?

Is this lead from an account with an active opportunity?

Has an AE worked this account recently?

Is another SDR working a different prospect at this account?

Is another SDR working a dupe of this prospect?

A few things might jump out at you right away. For one, many of those questions can't be answered by staying within *Leads*. Are they a customer? Is there an active opportunity? Is another AE/SDR working this account? Those questions require searching non-*Lead* objects—namely *Opportunities, Accounts*, and *Contacts*.

A fair bit of that detective work could be eliminated by moving SDR workflow from siloed *Leads* into the interconnected *Accounts & Contacts*. Before dumping *Leads* entirely, let's weigh the pitfalls as well as the advantages. Like the great American thinker Rory Gilmore of Gilmore Girls fame, when in doubt I turn to a pro-con list (see figure 3.1 below).

LEADS: PROs	LEADS: CONs
Great for transactional selling	Incomplete for complex B2B selling
Keeps the deadwood and non-*sales-ready* prospects in a silo	Splits your database into *Leads* and "everything else"
Clear line-in-the sand separation between marketing "suspects," active prospects and customers	A struggle to manage multiple prospects at *one company* simultaneously

Built-in web-to-lead and lead assignment rules	Difficult to measure progress with an account-based mindset
Works well when targeting prospect sequentially (first the CEO, then VP Sales, then HR, etc.)	Difficult to see prior conversations and history at a given company
Relatively harmless dumping ground for big, cold list imports	Increases time required for pre-call research
Out of the box, ease of lead-to-opportunity reporting	If a *Lead* is re-qualified, excluded from normal reporting

Figure 3.1 – Leads: Pro-Con list

The final item on the *pro* list makes the strongest case to my mind.

Out of the box, Salesforce reporting on converted leads is convenient. You can report on *Leads* created in a certain timeframe, group by lead source, and compare conversion rate and pipeline sourced (the dark and light bars in figure 3.2).

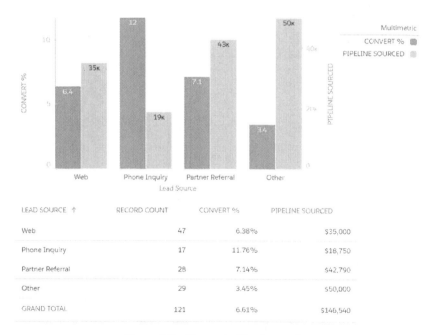

LEAD SOURCE ↑	RECORD COUNT	CONVERT %	PIPELINE SOURCED
Web	47	6.38%	$35,000
Phone Inquiry	17	11.76%	$18,750
Partner Referral	28	7.14%	$42,790
Other	29	3.45%	$50,000
GRAND TOTAL	121	6.61%	$146,540

Figure 3.2 – Converted lead reporting

I must admit, that's one nice looking report! Although we can build something similar with *Accounts & Contacts* (as you'll see in part 5), it's custom and requires configuration.

I asked my friend and fellow Salesforce MVP, Rebecca Dente, about this point. "Marketing cares a lot about contribution and pipeline metrics. They don't care about which objects are or aren't involved. It isn't 'lead object to opportunity object' data they're looking for. For most marketers, it's conversion rate, opportunity creation, and pipeline reporting. We can give them those metrics *and* make SDRs' lives easier, outside of leads."

I'll admit, I was slow to come around to the #NeverLeads movement. I understand why many companies opt to stick with using *Leads* despite the drawbacks. But to my mind, there is one instance where the pros are overwhelmingly in favor of using *Leads:*

▶ When generating high volumes of inbound leads

And two other instances when it's beyond debate that SDRs should be working *Accounts & Contacts*.

▶ When specializing roles with Inbound and Outbound SDRs

▶ When the selling strategy is account-based

Before sharing more on those instances, I should restate that #NeverLeads isn't my literal position. The *Leads* object should still be used as a staging area for web-to-lead, imports, and marketing automation. But there comes a point when a human should be "working" a record, that is when using *Accounts & Contacts* better serves the organization. There are several AppExchange Apps that automate the conversion. Or you can deploy custom code. A simple, if slightly tedious, option is to have your SDRs manually convert each *Lead* before they start to work with them. You want to leave your users with a bright, clear dividing line separating sales-worthy prospects from those that aren't yet sales-ready.

Generating High-Volume Inbound (Pro Leads)

If your company is generating a high-volume of inbound leads and/or your sales process is relatively simple/transactional, working *Leads* simplifies things. As an example, say you offer online scheduling software for small businesses. You might be generating thousands of free trial requests a month. Perhaps four out of five prospects that register actually follow through and activate the trial. And maybe only half of those ever log in two or more times. Are you willing to generate a thousand new *Accounts* each month if only one to two hundred ever enter a real evaluation process?

If you engage, qualify, and close a single buyer in a relatively high-velocity sales cycle, you can use Salesforce as designed. Take advantage of the pros and keep *Accounts & Contacts* the domain of active prospects and customers.

Specializing with Outbound SDRs (Con Leads)

An SDR tasked with qualifying inbound inquiries can work exclusively in *Leads*. It's unlikely that multiple prospects from one company will come inbound at *exactly* the same time. It is easy enough to do a quick dupe check and the flat nature of the lead record makes working a single prospect simple enough.

For SDRs chartered with outbound prospecting however, working *Leads* is not an option. Literally, it is an option of course. Just as, literally, SDRs could still do their jobs if you remove all the vowel keys from their keyboards. But they shouldn't have to.

I asked Jay Schmidt, Inside Sales Manager at Signiant, for his thoughts. "Managing the break between leads and contacts can be a struggle. When should a lead become a contact? Should a contact ever go back and re-start as a lead? Having that cold, hard division also assumes that reps are going do some copying, pasting, and searching to figure out if a lead is already a customer or if that lead's boss is being worked by another rep."

It's the nature of modern sales that buying decisions are often made as a committee. Which is just a fancy way of saying that any number of people are authorized to say *no* but it takes a small battalion of nodding heads to issue a single *yes*. With outbound prospecting, it is nearly impossible to work a single prospect and effectively generate opportunity. Reps are trying to generate interest and book a meeting at that company. A single "not interested" does little to discourage a good outbound SDR. I call this being *account-oriented*. You are focused on engaging, qualifying, and closing the account—not a single prospect.

Often, I see inbound SDRs working primarily within *Leads*. While outbound SDRs live in *Accounts & Contacts*. That is a fair compromise, provided you build in advanced lead routing (see chapter 4) to save reps time and prevent the inevitable turmoil from reps failing to properly check for existing *Leads, Contacts, Accounts,* and *Opportunities*.

If you've taken a fully *account-oriented* posture, or if your SDRs are bouncing back and forth between *Leads* and *Accounts & Contacts*, it is time to break the habit and leave *Leads* behind. As with many things that make users lives easier, this taxes sales ops and admins more heavily. Account dupes (e.g., Salesforce, Salesforce.com, SalesForce, etc.) are particularly destructive and need to be consistently cleaned and merged. As of the spring '16 release, we have native Data.com Duplicate Management to assist in policing these issues.

Going Account-Based (Con Leads)

"Account-Based Marketing" is white-hot right now. In case you're unfamiliar with the term, the best definition I've seen comes from Engagio CEO Jon Miller:

> *"The goal of an account-based process is to optimize your sales and marketing resources – time, headcount and budget – by focusing them on the accounts most likely to drive big revenue."*

Going "account-based" works best when specifically, or exclusively, targeting a defined universe of prospects. Rather than the high-volume and high-churn of SMB companies, an account-based strategy focuses on a finite and (mostly) fixed list of prospect accounts. Examples might include state governments, national grocery chains, $1B+ pharmaceutical companies, publicly traded software companies, etc. In these instances, *Accounts & Contacts* are a much easier path to follow.

The yardstick in account-based marketing and sales isn't the number of leads converted or a certain lead conversion rate. It's about account coverage, engagement, and pipeline. At the end of the day, very few B2B companies sell to an individual. It's all about the account. Never more so than when talking an account-based strategy. Jim McDonough, VP of Sales at Threat Stack, put it this way: "When targeting strategic accounts, you think in terms of accounts, not individual prospects. Your SDRs are prospecting strategic accounts. Your AEs are presenting to strategic accounts. Your marketing is focused on strategic accounts. Instead of having your reps live and work in a 'single person at a time' view, bring it all to the account level."

CHAPTER 4

⚡

FLOW PROSPECTS TO REPS

WHETHER AN SDR is assigned a new prospect as a *Lead* or a *Contact*, there's one thing we can all agree on: *the goal is assigning to the right person, the first time.* For a brand new company, this is easy. Did you generate an inbound lead from the Northeast? Excellent, assign it to Clint Connecticut. Another from the Southeast? Great! Give it to Flora Florida. A third from Canada? Route that one over to Martin Mapleleaf. And on and on.

These familiar lead assignment rules are native to Salesforce (figure 4.1).

Figure 4.1 – Lead assignment rules

But what if you aren't a brand-new company? Returning to our inbound lead example from chapter 2, the SDR pre-flight checklist includes:

▶ Is this lead from a current customer?

▶ Is this lead from an account with an active opportunity?

▶ Has an AE worked this account recently?

▶ Is another SDR working a different prospect at this account?

▶ Is another SDR working a dupe of this prospect?

In an ideal world, your SDRs wouldn't have to do all that detective work before picking up the phone. In many orgs, it takes a double major in forensic archeology and investigative journalism just to decipher a single account's history with your company.

Fundamentally, there is no point in sending every *sales-ready* lead to an SDR and leaving it to them to re-route if necessary. It is embarrassing when an SDR calls a current customer with no knowledge of the existing relationship. It is frustrating when an SDR calls the decision maker in an active opportunity and appears clueless as to the existing level of engagement. And it is likely to breed mutiny when an SDR calls a company currently being worked by another SDR or an AE.

Manny Alamwala, a Business Development Associate at Vision Critical put it to me this way. "Every outbound rep loves it when an account they are working comes inbound. Ideally, that new activity should alert the existing outbound account owner. Time is so much of the essence in following up on inbound leads. You can't afford to lose time shuffling the lead between reps. That process needs to be automated."

You can have all the rules, procedures, and processes you want to avoid *channel conflict* between SDRs. But if diligent and thorough searching in Salesforce is where the rubber meets the road, you're going to have problems.

Mercifully, there's a simple way to handle this.

Once a prospect has been deemed *sales-ready*, we can let Salesforce do the heavy lifting of routing them. A relatively new tool, Visual Workflow, can do things that would have required custom code (or a terribly bored intern) just a few years ago.

In case you are unfamiliar, Salesforce bills Visual Workflow this way:

Visual Workflow lets you automate business processes by building flows and distributing them to the right users or systems. A flow is an application that can execute logic, interact with the Salesforce database, call Apex classes, and collect data from users.

With Workflow Rules, and even Process Builder (workflow version 2.0), there are still many things that can't be done declaratively. If 80% of your needs could be satisfied with clicks, that meant 20% remained the domain of developers and code. Visual Workflow has pushed that "code cliff" back significantly. I don't believe that code's days are numbered by any stretch. But I do know that with a little study, any admin can do amazing things with flows.

A Better Flow for Lead Assignment

Before you jump into configuration, you'll want to map out the different scenarios. In figure 4.2 below, I've shared a simplified example.

IF THIS	THEN THAT
Lead is from a current customer	Route to the customer success or account manager
Lead is from an account with an active opportunity	Route to the opportunity owner
An AE worked this account within the last six months	Route to the account executive
Another SDR is working a different prospect at this account	Route to that SDR
Okay, all's clear!	Route to the Inbound SDR Queue

Figure 4.2 – Lead assignment mapping

As I mentioned earlier, relying on reps to deep search and re-route is overly optimistic. Most inbound SDRs are facing Marketing Service Level Agreements (SLAs) that specify time-to-first attempt. And to be honest, searching Salesforce is tedious. A better approach is to let Visual Workflow do the heavy lifting for you. A good flow beats leaving it to reps to properly search and re-route records all day every day.

Figure 4.3 represents one way of using Visual Workflow to assign *Leads*. (*Admin Note*: this is an autolaunched flow called by Process Builder.) The linked YouTube video will give you a walkthrough and explanation (http://sdrbook.io/flowmqls - all lowercase).

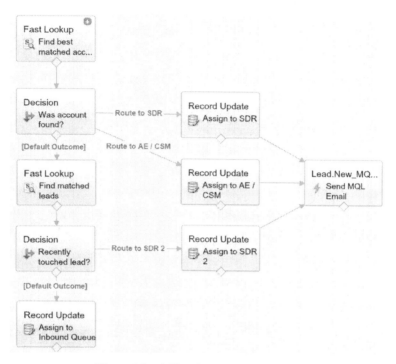

Figure 4.3 – A Flow for lead assignment

Are you with me so far?

To review, the flow is handling all the logic and decision trees. It operates much like a process flowchart—taking action based on logic. Now, what I've failed to mention up to this point is exactly *how* our flow is finding records from the same company. I've tried different approaches with different clients. While not 100% perfect, here's the best solution I've found to date: *domain formula fields*.

Nearly every single prospect passed by marketing to your SDRs will have an email address. The overwhelming majority of those will be corporate domains (i.e., non-Hotmail, Yahoo, Gmail, etc.). Using a custom formula field, you can extract the domain from that email address:

```
IF(
    CONTAINS(Email, "gmail") ||
    CONTAINS(Email, "yahoo") ||
    CONTAINS(Email, "hotmail") ||
    CONTAINS(Email, "outlook"),
    NULL,
    SUBSTITUTE(Email, LEFT(Email, FIND( "@", Email)), NULL)
)
```

This formula essentially says, if it isn't personal email, return the string after the @ symbol. Your **Email Domain** field should give you results similar to figure 4.4 below.

My New MQLs ▼

NAME ↑	COMPANY	EMAIL	EMAIL DOMAIN
Acton Obrien	Nisi Institute	actono@nisiinst.com	nisiinst.com
Andy Young	Dickenson plc	a_young@dickenson.com	dickenson.com
Bertha Boxer	Farmers Coop. of Florida	bertha@fcof.net	fcof.net
Betty Bair	American Banking Corp.	bblair@abankingco.com	abankingco.com
Bill Dadio Jr	Zenith Electronics	bill.dadio@zenith.com	zenith.com
Brenda Mcclure	Cadinal Inc.	brenda@cardinal.net	cardinal.net
Brian Brian	hubspot	asdasdsd@hubspot.com	hubspot.com
Carolyn Crens...	Ace Iron and Steel Inc.	carolync@aceis.com	aceis.com
David Monaco	Blues Entertainment Co...	david@blues.com	blues.com
Eugena Luce	Pacific Retail Group	eluce@pacificretail.com	pacificretail.com
Gillian Madill	Salesforce	notjill@salesforce.com	salesforce.com

Figure 4.4 – Email domains

To identify matching companies, we need to add a similar field on *Accounts*. You can make the website field required on *Accounts* and then create a **Company Domain** custom formula field as follows:

27

```
IF(
  CONTAINS(Website, "www."),
  MID(Website, FIND("www.", Website, 1)+4, (LEN(Website) -
  FIND("www.", Website, 1)+4)),
  SUBSTITUTE(
    Website, LEFT(Website, FIND("http://", Website)+6),
    NULL)
  )
```

On *Accounts*, you'll be left with (figure 4.5):

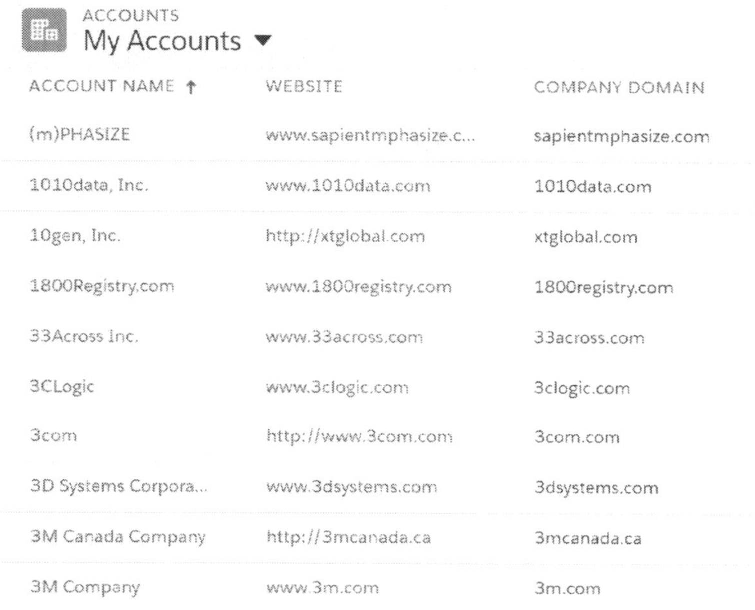

ACCOUNTS
My Accounts ▼

ACCOUNT NAME ↑	WEBSITE	COMPANY DOMAIN
(m)PHASIZE	www.sapientmphasize.c...	sapientmphasize.com
1010data, Inc.	www.1010data.com	1010data.com
10gen, Inc.	http://xtglobal.com	xtglobal.com
1800Registry.com	www.1800registry.com	1800registry.com
33Across Inc.	www.33across.com	33across.com
3CLogic	www.3clogic.com	3clogic.com
3com	http://www.3com.com	3com.com
3D Systems Corpora...	www.3dsystems.com	3dsystems.com
3M Canada Company	http://3mcanada.ca	3mcanada.ca
3M Company	www.3m.com	3m.com

Figure 4.5 – Company domains

These two fields are the power behind the matching. A new *Lead* from marc@salesforce.com will match with the *Account* whose **Website** is http://www.salesforce.com. The queries, logical branches, ownership changes, and email alerts are handled within the flow. The linked YouTube video will give you a walkthrough (http://sdrbook.io/flowmqls - all lowercase).

I'll admit this approach is more complicated than native lead assignment rules. And the **Email Domain** and **Company Domain** solution isn't bulletproof. But I'm not one to let the perfect be the enemy of the good. I've found this approach works well for most. But you can add sophistication with more complex matching rules as your organization's needs dictate.

CHAPTER 5

⚡

BUILD IN GUARDRAILS

IMAGINE THE FOLLOWING SCENARIO:

▶ An outbound SDR targets Danielle Morrill, CEO & Cofounder of Mattermark.

▶ Danielle doesn't return the calls and emails.

▶ Ten days after the SDR's final email, Joshua Adragna, Mattermark's Director of Sales, becomes an inbound lead.

Who gets to work that account? What happens if the inbound SDR books the meeting? Does the outbound rep lose out on the credit and the commission?

"You have to have touch rules in place to address when an SDR can go after a company that's already in the database," shared Kevin Dorsey, VP of Sales at SnackNation. "Rather than having reps navigate all these if/then rules themselves, it's better to just build it into Salesforce. So when a rep sees an account, it's either *red light* or *green light*. If there's another lead from this company that's been touched in the past fifteen days, *red light*. If not, *green light*. Something that simple can be a game changer."

It is often the case that an outbound SDR can create awareness and interest within an account without ever speaking with a prospect. It is reasonable to assume this is caused by an inbound marketing response following closely on the heels of outbound activity. To address this scenario, you need to build in guardrails to prevent channel conflict. The lead routing flow presented in the previous chapter is one way of handling this. Alternately or additionally, you can create a visual signal to alert reps before potential overlap becomes a major problem.

Adding an SDR Signal

First, we need a way to flag if an account has had an activity within a certain time period—say the last 30 days. Second, when a *Lead* is assigned to an inbound SDR, we need Salesforce to surface that indicator.

We can accomplish the first with a formula field and the second with an autolaunched flow. To set the **SDR Signal**, you'll create a custom image formula field on *Accounts* using the record's last activity date and a custom picklist field called **Account Status** (more on that in chapter 8).

```
IF(
  ISPICKVAL(Account_Status__c,"Open")
  ||
  LastActivityDate + 30 < TODAY(),
  IMAGE("/logos/Standard/task/logo.svg", "Green light", 20, 20),
  IMAGE("/logos/Custom/Triangle_Red/logo.png", "Red light", 20, 20)
  )
```

This formula says that if either the **Account Status** is "Open" or the **Last Activity Date** was more than thirty days ago, show the green checkbox icon. Otherwise, show the red triangle one. Note: these images are already included within Salesforce. Just add /logos/ to the end of your Salesforce URL and you'll find a bunch to choose from (e.g., https://na##.salesforce.com/logos/). Also, specifying height and width to 20px by 20px makes it look nice and tidy on the page layout.

Let's return to the Mattermark example from the start of this chapter. When the inbound SDR goes to the Mattermark account, they would see the **SDR Signal** was red and know to route the lead to the **SDR Owner** (see figure 5.1).

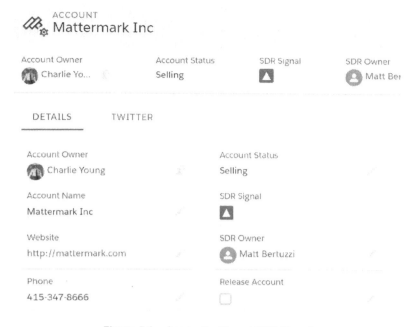

Figure 5.1 – Account with red SDR Signal

This is the first step. If an SDR were to visit the Mattermark record, they would see that the **SDR Signal** was a red triangle—signifying that another rep was working this account. But as we covered earlier, you want to limit reliance on SDRs searching Salesforce. Via automation, we want to bring that *Account* information onto the *Lead* record where an inbound SDR is likely working.

You'll use an autolaunched flow to do this. You'll want to create a custom lookup field called **Best Matched Account** on the *Lead* object. This field will hold the value of a matched account—should one be found—right on the *Lead* itself. Figure 5.2 below presents one way of using flow to populate this field. When a *Lead* is assigned to an inbound SDR, a Process Builder would kick off and call the flow.

Figure 5.2 – Best matched account flow

The flow would then search for *Accounts* where the **Company Domain** matches the **Email Domain** from the *Lead*. If a match is found, the **Best Matched Account** field on *Leads* is updated. The linked YouTube video will give you a walkthrough and explanation (http://sdrbook.io/bestmatched - all lowercase).

Let's return to our Mattermark example to see how this looks to a rep. When the inbound SDR views Joshua Adragna's *Lead*, she can hover over the **Best Matched Account** to see Mattermark's **SDR Signal** and **SDR Owner** fields (see figure 5.3).

Figure 5.3 – Hover over best matched account

That red indicator lets her know that an outbound SDR is currently working Mattermark. And that she should reassign the inbound lead to him or her. These guardrails add real value to your users. They also help to prevent the bad blood and ill will that can result from channel conflict. I can't recommend them highly enough.

Limit How Many Accounts an SDR Can Own

I recently came across a question on the answers board of the Salesforce

Success Community (https://success.salesforce.com/answers). An admin asked if "there is a way I can modify a validation rule to give off an error when a user tries to change ownership to themselves and they already own more than 125 accounts. We are trying to limit our reps to only own 125 at a time."

This isn't an uncommon need with outbound SDR teams. Often, to encourage focus, leadership will cap the number of accounts a single rep can own. Reps have a natural, human tendency to hoard and land grab prospects (think: bread and milk before a big storm). Account coverage suffers when reps have more accounts than they can reasonably work. And if your growth plans include hiring more reps, you'll have to endure the painful process of clawing back accounts. Not fun!

There's a reasonably simple solution that allows you to cap account ownership.

The first step is to create a custom numeric field on the *User* object called **# Accounts Owned**. The goal is that every time an SDR takes ownership of a new account, automation will increment that field by one. Conversely, every time an SDR *gives up* ownership of an account, you'll want to reduce that field by one. One final consideration is that you'll have to populate the **# of Accounts Owned** fields before turning to automation. Sadly, these tools don't fire retroactively.

To build the automation, I recommend a Process Builder with two nodes. The first node will increment the **# of Accounts Owned** field by one when an *Account* is taken. You'll want to make sure that it fires *both* when the **SDR Owner** field is changed *and* when a new record is created. To accomplish this, set the criteria to the following formula:

```
NOT(ISBLANK([Account].SDR_Owner__c )) &&
(ISCHANGED([Account].SDR_Owner__c ) || ISNEW())
```

For the update action, you'll span to the User record and set the field value with the formula below. You are simply taking the old value and adding one to it.

```
[Account].SDR_Owner__c.of_Accounts__c +1
```

The second node will handle reducing the **# of Accounts Owned** field when an *Account* is given up. This is slightly more complicated. You can't span to the previous *User* of the **SDR Owner** field once it has been blanked out or changed to someone else. To address this, I recommend you create a **Release Account** checkbox field. If an SDR wants to give up an account, they just check the box and automation does the rest (see figure 5.4 below).

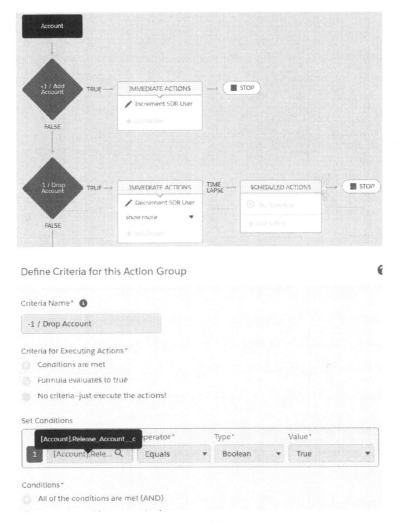

Figure 5.4 – Number of *Accounts* process

For this node, you'll create two immediate actions. The first action will span to the *User* and set the **# of Accounts Owned** field value with this formula:

```
[Account].SDR_Owner__c.of_Accounts__c -1
```

We are reducing the current total by one. The second action will blank out the **SDR Owner** field and uncheck the **Release Account** checkbox. The linked YouTube video will give you a walkthrough and explanation (http://sdrbook.io/limitonaccounts - all lowercase).

All of this might seem like overkill. But trust me, giving your reps the ability to scan a "My Accounts" list view and release Accounts without clicking into each and every record, will earn you major sales ops karma points. The final step is to add a Validation Rule on *Accounts*. If your goal was to limit reps to 350 accounts, the validation rule would be:

```
SDR_Owner__r.of_Accounts__c >= 350
```

When an SDR has fewer than three hundred fifty accounts, they'll be able to take ownership with ease and you'll be able to report on the count behind the scenes. When they try to add the 351st account, they'll be presented with the following error (see figure 5.5).

Figure 5.5 – Over limit validation rule

Easy peasy.

Okay, let's recap. So far we've used custom formula fields to match prospect emails and company websites. Then we leveraged autolaunched flows to route new leads to the correct owner—be they a Customer Success Manager, Account Executive, or SDR. Next, we built in guardrails to make sure that the left hand (reps working in *Leads*) knows what the right hand (reps working *Accounts & Contacts*) is doing. Then, we designed a way to limit the number of accounts one SDR can own.

Now, it's time to make sure prospects are assigned to the correct reps. For many SDR teams, and for the vast majority of inbound SDR teams, this means round-robin lead assignment. By that I mean distributing prospects evenly and in turn across a team. That's exactly what we'll cover in the next chapter.

CHAPTER 6

⚡

SPIN LEADS RIGHT ROUND

WE AT THE BRIDGE GROUP, INC. publish research on B2B companies with sales development groups. I know from our recent *SDR Metrics & Compensation Report* (http://sdrbook.io/SDRMETRICS) that more than 30% of companies have moved away from traditional territories for SDRs and implemented round-robin assignment or shark tanks/open pools. For groups focused on inbound qualification, the percentage using round-robin doubled to 60%.

I'm a big believer in round robin lead distribution. It levels the playing field for SDRs and AEs alike. Say you have two SDRs and two AEs paired one-to-one. Maybe AE #1 is brand new and she doesn't care about high degrees of qualification. She just wants at-bats and will take any meeting she can get. While perhaps AE #2 has a very fat territory and will only consider supremely qualified meetings. From the perspective of meetings passed, the SDR for the AE #1 looks like a hero. While the SDR for AE #2, although producing the same number of meetings, appears to be significantly underperforming. Is that setting each SDR rep up evenly for success?

Or consider it from the AE's perspective. Say SDR #1 gets promoted and now AE #1 doesn't have anyone setting meetings for her. Even once a new SDR is hired, they still have the onboarding and ramp period until they are back to steady state. Is that fair to the AE?

Finally, inbound leads are stubborn animals. They simply refuse to present themselves in equitable shares for each territory. Say the vast majority of your leads are from technology companies—which are heavily weighted toward the Eastern and Western United States. That could leave your central territory with significantly lower lead volume. Is that equitable?

If you have no interest in adjudicating disputes over AE and/or SDR quality, round robin lead distribution is a simple and fair solution.

The Leaky Lead Sprinkler

The classic approach for round-robin is "lead sprinkler" lead assignment. This approach uses an auto number on *Leads* and a custom formula field. Imagine that you have three inbound SDRs. Salesforce would automatically generate an incrementing number field. Then, you would create a **Round Robin ID** field using the formula:

```
MOD(
   VALUE(Lead_Number__c), 3
   ) +1
```

This would return 1, 2, or 3 based on the auto number (see figure 6.1)

Lead Number	Round-Robin ID
21	1
22	2
23	3
24	1
25	2
26	3

Figure 6.1 – Auto number formula results

This solution works perfectly . . . until it doesn't. The biggest issue with this approach is that auto number fields are, by definition, automatic. You can't exclude certain records from receiving an auto number. Say your marketing automation system mistakenly creates two duplicate records. You discover the error and delete them. As a result, two reps have been skipped in the rotation.

Compound this import after import and manual record creation after creation and you can end up with a significant skew. Over time, I've seen sheer randomness "shortchange" SDRs by five to ten percent fewer leads. What you really want is to *conditionally* auto number.

Conditional Auto Numbering

David Litton is a Solutions Architect at Ad Victorian Solutions. On his blog, *Salesforce Sidekick*, he details a solution leveraging Process Builder. (https://salesforcesidekick.com/2016/06/27/how-to-create-a-conditional-auto-number-with-just-process-builder/)

In short, David's approach (figure 6.2 below) uses a custom object with its own auto number field and two Process Builders: one to generate the auto number and a second to add it to the *Lead*.

Figure 6.2 – Conditional auto-number process

For our purposes, you would slightly alter David's steps as follows:

- ▶ A lead status is changed to *MQL*
- ▶ Which kicks off Process Builder #1 to call the *Lead Assignment* flow
- ▶ The flow finds no existing accounts or leads and assigns the lead to the *New MQL* queue
- ▶ Which kicks off Process Builder #2 to create a new record on the custom object with an auto number
- ▶ Which kicks off Process Builder #3 and, based on the **Round Robin ID** formula field, assigns it to the correct inbound SDR (see figure 6.3 below)

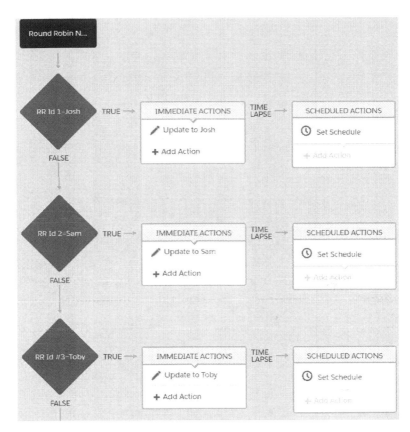

Figure 6.3 – Process to update *Lead* via custom object

Phew. There's a lot going on there. The linked YouTube video will give you a walkthrough and explanation (http://sdrbook.io/roundrobins - all lowercase).

You don't have to follow this exact approach to sprinkle leads in a round robin fashion. If you like, you can rely on the traditional **Round Robin ID** field on *Leads*. Just be aware, without these extra steps it's likely that your distribution won't be one hundred percent even. If you do elect to stick with the simpler approach, let me make one recommendation. For your highest value leads, build in the extra work to ensure equity.

Maybe it's *Contact Us* leads. Or perhaps it's *Demo Requests*. Whatever the source, I can promise you that every SDR has a highly-attuned Spidey-sense when it comes to fair distribution of "good leads." If the round-robin sprinkling of these starts to skew, you'll hear about it.

CHAPTER 7

⚡

FLAG HIGH-PRIORITY LEADS

THERE IS A LOT OF EMPHASIS on lead response time for SDRs. InsideSales.com's *Lead Response Management Study* found a five-minute response means you're four times more likely to qualify that lead than a ten-minute response, and more than twenty times more likely than after a thirty-minute wait. That's pretty persuasive.

But of everyone who submits a form on your website, a fair portion are likely top of funnel prospects—ebook downloaders, webinar registrants, etc. Every lead doesn't necessarily deserve an equal application of resources. Committing your reps to calling each and every prospect within five minutes is both technically challenging and, to my mind, prioritizing *fast outreach* over *prepared outreach*. You don't want anyone with internet access and a pulse to drive the SDR team's activity.

I recommend breaking leads into two categories: high-priority and other. For high-priority leads, the focus is on speed-to-assignment, speed-to-notification, and speed-to-contact. For the remainder of leads, I like to trust in the SDRs themselves to work them in a timely manner. Or, if necessary, you can build in a "clawback and re-distribute" for any records that don't meet the Service Level Agreement (discussed below).

Mallory Lee is an ExactTarget-alum, marketing operations pro, and consultant to high-growth marketing organizations. "I don't know many reps who'll complain about too many high-value leads in their funnel," she commented. "The lead follow-up SLA is usually just 'as fast as possible.' With my teams in the past, if a hot lead came in, reps were allowed to step out of any meeting, head back to their desks, and reach out. Everyone understood that

that part of the business takes priority."

The challenge for us in sales operations is to balance notifying reps of new leads and alerting them to high-priority (get up and go!) leads. Let's be honest, flooding a rep's inbox with new lead emails can be a distraction. That's why I recommend taking a *notify on high-priority only* approach. Kyle Smith is an inside sales consultant on my team. I asked him to share his philosophy on notification. "Don't send an email for each new lead. First, it pulls reps out of Salesforce. And second, if they glance at their phone notification, it's too easy to get distracted by Twitter, Facebook, etc. Most reps refresh their list views religiously and won't ever miss a new lead."

"But for high-value leads, go all out. An email plus a push notification plus a text message isn't too much," he added. "What high-value means varies from company to company—maybe it's contact us, start a trial, or request a demo. For these leads, time is of the essence."

In working with SDR teams, I found that the best ways to get their attention are *text, push notification, unread items icon, then email* in that order. There's an easy way to get all three out of four: Chatter.

You can use Process Builder to at mention the **Lead Owner** on the record's Chatter feed. This does three things at once (see figure 7.1):

1. It sends an email of the Chatter post and links to the record.
2. It displays a notification alert in Salesforce.
3. It sends a push notification on Salesforce1 (the mobile app).

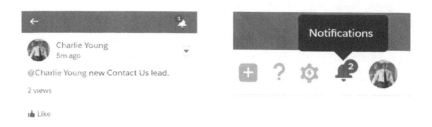

Figure 7.1 – Three flavors of notification

That should be enough to get just about any rep's attention. Note: this assumes that your organization has enable in-app and push notification, that your users have Salesforce1 (the mobile app) installed, and that their Chatter *Email Notifications* are turned on. You should work to enable all three. In my experience, Chatter on Salesforce1 is a great way to increase user engagement.

The key to any "red alert" system is that it can't become routine. If you define your high-priority threshold too low, reps might receive these alerts upwards of ten times a day. If these notifications become normalized, they can blend into the routine of the day and become easy to ignore. You'll want to ensure that notifications are rare and respected.

Chatter, Email, and the Nuclear Option

If you're still concerned about high-priority leads going cold, there are a few additional steps you can take. I worked with one client that took a "Chatter then email then nuclear" approach. Their philosophy was after an hour of in-activity, the rep got a nudge. But after three hours, they got a smack.

For this client, as part of the Process Builder that posts to Chatter, we created additional scheduled actions.

- ▶ After 1 hour with an unchanged **Lead Status**, a reminder email was sent and the SDR Manager was alerted via Chatter
- ▶ After 3 hours with an unchanged **Lead Status**, the record was ripped away and returned to the Inbound SDR Queue

Harsh, but fair. In Process Builder, this would look like figure 7.2 below:

Figure 7.2 – High-priority process

This might be overkill for your organization. But if you are serious about quick response to high-priority leads, this is the type of "encouragement" that every new SDR only needs to experience once.

If you do follow this process, I recommend excluding any leads assigned on Friday, Saturday, or Sunday. There's no need to punish a rep for failing to respond at 8PM Friday night or 6AM Sunday morning. I'll often use a formula similar to this:

```
CASE(
    MOD(MQL_Date__c - DATE(1900, 1, 7), 7),
    1, "On", 2, "On", 3, "On", 4, "On",
    "Off"
    )
```

This takes the date the lead was assigned (in Greenwich Mean Time) and returns "On" for Monday-Thursday and "Off" for Friday-Sunday. If you want to get more granular and work in the hour that the record was assigned, you can. But that makes you far braver and more dedicated than I.

Bubble up Reheated Prospects

One final thing you might want to consider is when to re-MQL previously "recycled" prospects. I've seen many marketing teams deploy "a beautiful mind"-level lead scoring rule to determine when a recycled prospect is, once again, sales-ready. And I've seen SDRs barely glance at those leads. "I talked to them awhile back, there's nothing there," they say. SDRs are dismissive, marketing is irked, and nobody wins.

One approach is to re-"MQL" prospects when something suggests they've taking a step forward in their buying process. Zoe Silverman, Sales Operations Manager at Yesware, shared her philosophy with me. "Understanding and mapping out your customers' buyer journey is key. You want to be able to monitor where your prospects are within that journey inside Salesforce. Often, companies model based on what they think is happening at a given prospect. That doesn't always accurately reflect what they're really going through. In the very early stages, when you haven't even had a first call, that might be marketing or digital behavior."

Zoey's comment started me thinking about ways to infer when a prospect crosses an invisible gate in their journey and how to flag the appropriate SDR to take action. Think about the content and marketing resources that are available on your website. I suspect that most of those are TOFU (top of the funnel) offers—ebooks, webinars, explainer videos, and so on.

But perhaps you have one or two pieces that suggest a prospect isn't *just researching*, but maybe *accessing* these pieces, indicating they might have taken a step forward. Examples might include ROI calculators, a competitive comparison matrix, or a guide on how to sell your tool to the C-suite. If you've deployed marketing automation software, this is an instance where you might bypass all the scoring rules, sound the alarm, and alert the appropriate rep. But if you haven't deployed marketing automation, you can use Process Builder to reach the same ends.

As a first step, you can add a **Funnel Stage** picklist on the *Campaign* object. You might use values such as "Top," "Middle," "Bottom," and so on to indicate where the content falls. Imagine that one of your bottom of the funnel content pieces is a "Bullet-Proof ROI Workbook" (figure 7.3 below):

CAMPAIGN
Bullet-Proof ROI Workbook

Type	Start Date	Content Link	Campaign Brief
Ebook	11/1/2016	https://drive.google.com...	https://docs.google.com/docu...

RELATED   DETAILS

Campaign Name
Bullet-Proof ROI Workbook

Campaign Owner
Matt Bertuzzi

Type
Ebook

Active
☑

Start Date
11/1/2016

End Date

Content Link
https://drive.google.com/open?
id=1iFbbmrn6uA7ZJs40-XvEob9T

Status
In Progress

Campaign Brief
https://docs.google.com/document/d/13iVGhJxiB
o7vcC46nrv-CKVUVctt3TbXAjpm

Funnel Stage
Bottom

Figure 7.3 – Campaign funnel stage

Next, you can create a Process Builder off the *Campaign Member* object. Each time a campaign member is created—where the linked *Campaign* has "Bottom" as the **Funnel Stage** and the linked *Contact* has either "Early" or "Middle" as the **Journey Stage**—the Process will fire. You might use an email alert to send a templated notification to the *Contact's* owner (figure 7.4 below).

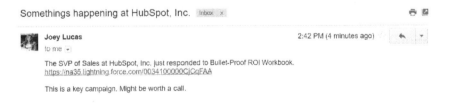

Somethings happening at HubSpot, Inc.   Inbox x

Joey Lucas   2:42 PM (4 minutes ago)
to me

The SVP of Sales at HubSpot, Inc. just responded to Bullet-Proof ROI Workbook.
https://na35.lightning.force.com/0034100000CjCqFAA

This is a key campaign. Might be worth a call.

Figure 7.4 – Journey stage alert email

I'm sure you can think of any number of additional use cases—Data.com reports the contact is promoted, a technographic tool like Datanyze updates the "technologies in use," and so on. If you don't have—or don't control—marketing automation, you can still bubble up key moments thanks to Process Builder.

PART 2

PLAN

If you're trying to persuade people to do something, it seems to me you should use their language, the language they use every day, the language in which they think.

—DAVID OGILVY

CHAPTER 8

⚡

PUT CONTEXT FRONT AND CENTER

IN PART 1, we worked our way through when it's appropriate to move away from *Leads* and toward *Accounts & Contacts*. We stepped through an SDR's thought process when first receiving a new prospect. We built guardrails to assure proper routing and avoid embarrassing missteps. Finally, we tackled round-robin lead assignment and ways to flag high-priority prospects.

Now, when one of your SDRs is assigned a prospect, they're ready to pick up the phone that very second and start selling, right?

SDR:	<Ding!> New lead. Let's do this! <Ring Ring>
PROSPECT:	Hello
SDR:	Hi {!FirstName} this is Elle Dior from SomeSoft. How are you?
PROSPECT:	Uh, I'm fi...
SDR:	Good, good. I saw you had some activity on our website and I wanted to reach out. What's your strategy today for achieving {!BigGenericGoal}?

Have you ever received that call?

I'm sorry to say I get at least two of those a week. If you're like me, when it happens you're thinking two things. One, why did I pick up my phone? And two, what can I say to end this call as quickly as possible?

I don't find anything offensive about receiving a prospecting call. SDRs gotta eat after all. But knowing I "did something" on a company's website is the opposite of a conversation starter. I recently ran across this line from Marc Jacobs, VP of Sales at Greenhouse Software: *"No prospect wants to talk to a rep who knows less than they do."*

#Truth.

When it comes to pre-call research, there are two types of SDRs: *the high-preparers* and the *high-actors*. High-preparers are like golfers standing over a putt. They must line it up, read the green, talk it over, squat, stand, and repeat. They'll act, but only when they're good and ready. High-actors, are an entirely different breed. Motion and improvisation are where they thrive. "If you do have someone who is more of a researcher, don't expect them to rush to the phone. That's not where they'll ever be comfortable. They excel at personalizing their outreach to prospects," shared Emma Lehman from Quota Factory. "If you have someone with a high activity drive, don't expect them to review marketing history and digest a prospect's last quarterly earnings report. They won't. Both profiles can get the job done, but you have to support them in different ways."

Emma makes a key point. Training reps to act against their DNA is a losing battle. I, for example, was a *high-preparer* SDR back in my day. Expecting me to make one hundred dials a day was as realistic as requiring me to make one hundred free-throws in a row with no misses.

Your goal with your reps should be to make Salesforce complement and support their selling styles. This means:

▶ Giving *high-researchers* faster access to key prospect intelligence. You want to speed up the time it takes for them to go through their pre-call research ritual.

▶ Giving *high-actors* the ability to quickly scan and glean "nuggets" for use in prospecting. You want to limit how deeply they have to dig. If it's more than a few clicks, they just won't do it.

For most sales development teams, it isn't a lack of data that's the problem. It's that there is too much. Over the next several chapters, we'll tackle customizing Salesforce for both SDR profiles. And we'll review ways to shorten the distance between valuable context and your reps' fingertips.

CHAPTER 9

⚡

ARCHITECT LEAD STATUSES

VIEWING A RECORD for the first time is like getting behind the wheel of someone else's car. It's familiar in that everything (steering wheel, mirrors, pedals) is in the same place, but it still takes a few moments to orient yourself. In my interviews with SDRs across companies and across industries, four key "orientation points" came up again and again. These are the pieces that *high-researchers* and *high-actors* alike pay attention to before making their first attempt. I've taken to calling these the 4Ls.

They include:

- ► Lead Status
- ► Last Campaign
- ► LinkedIn
- ► Location

Nearly every single SDR I spoke with listed these four pieces as central to their pre-call research process. Most reps had access to mountains of marketing automation details and a robust activity history, too. But they expressed rarely, if ever, finding anything useful buried there.

One SDR sent me a screenshot of a new inbound lead to emphasize this point (see figure 9.1 below).

Subject	Due Date ↓	Assigned To	Last Modified Date/Time
Opened Email: WB_L	10/5/2016	Sync, Marketo	10/19/2016 9:52 PM
Was Delivered Email:	10/4/2016	Sync, Marketo	10/19/2016 8:24 PM
Was Delivered Email:	9/29/2016	Sync, Marketo	10/15/2016 3:05 AM
Was Delivered Email:	9/25/2016	Sync, Marketo	10/14/2016 7:26 AM
Was Delivered Email:	9/22/2016	Sync, Marketo	10/7/2016 4:28 AM
Was Delivered Email:	9/20/2016	Sync, Marketo	10/6/2016 3:57 AM
Was Delivered Email:	9/19/2016	Sync, Marketo	9/28/2016 8:43 PM
Was Delivered Email:	9/18/2016	Sync, Marketo	9/27/2016 5:01 PM
Was Delivered Email:	9/14/2016	Sync, Marketo	9/22/2016 9:27 PM
Was Delivered Email:	9/13/2016	Sync, Marketo	9/18/2016 4:39 AM
Was Delivered Email:	9/11/2016	Sync, Marketo	9/16/2016 7:28 AM
Was Delivered Email:	8/18/2016	Sync, Marketo	9/4/2016 5:31 PM
Was Delivered Email:	8/11/2016	Sync, Marketo	9/4/2016 12:40 PM
Was Delivered Email:	8/9/2016	Sync, Marketo	9/4/2016 7:00 AM
Was Delivered Email:	8/4/2016	Sync, Marketo	8/30/2016 3:47 AM
Was Delivered Email:	7/31/2016	Sync, Marketo	8/29/2016 9:45 PM
Was Delivered Email:	7/29/2016	Sync, Marketo	8/27/2016 11:17 AM
Was Delivered Email:	7/27/2016	Sync, Marketo	8/27/2016 2:38 AM

Show me fewer ▲ records per list page

Figure 9.1 – Marketing automation matrix

"If you can pull anything useful out of that, you're my hero," he added. "It's like staring into the Matrix."

Indeed it is.

Simplifying Lead Status

Let's look at the 4Ls in order, starting with Lead Status.

One of my favorite features of working *Leads* in the Lightning is Path. In case you aren't familiar, you can compare the **Lead Status** picklist experience (in Classic) to Path (in Lightning) in figure 9.2 below. Note, today Path is available for *Leads*, *Opportunities*, and custom objects. Expansion to all objects is listed on the roadmap.

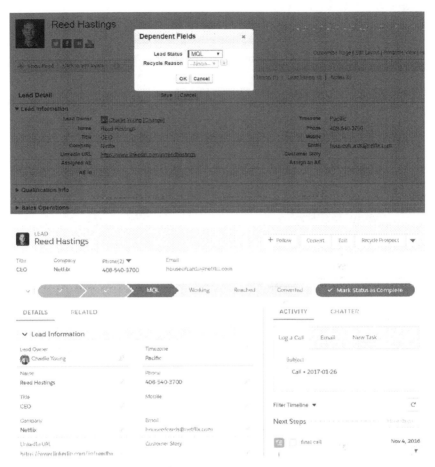

Figure 9.2 – Classic (top) compared to Lightning (bottom)

It is *a lot* easier to orient in the *distance-to-goal* visual of Path than with the standard picklist approach in Classic. Additionally, specific fields and text guidance can be presented below each "stage" in Path (which we'll cover in chapter 13).

As a first step, my advice is to limit the number of lead statuses for SDR-owned prospects to six or fewer. This isn't a hard-and-fast rule, but try to avoid the temptation of over-engineering here. The statuses I've found most widely applicable are:

▶ **Rejected**- not a real lead

▶ **Recycled**- returning to nurture/marketing

▶ **MQL**- Marketing Qualified Lead, shorthand for sales-ready

▶ **Working**- SDR is making outreach attempts

▶ **Reached**- SDR has had 1+ conversation(s) with the prospect

▶ **Qualified**- passed to an AE as an introductory meeting or qualified opportunity

In many Salesforce instances, the line between "Rejected" and "Recycled" is often muddied. But it needn't be.

SDRs should only reject prospects that aren't real buyers (students, competitors, fake names, countries you don't service, etc.) "Moe Szyslak" at Moe's Tavern? Reject the lead. "Jessica Jones" at Alias Investigations? Reject the lead. "Titus Andromedon" at Pinot Noir, Inc.? You get the idea.

Your reps should recycle prospects they haven't been able to reach or have reached and remain unqualified. Recycling a prospect isn't a "ding" against marketing. Even the highest performing sales development teams recycle more leads than they qualify. "There's a very clear line between what rejected and recycled means in terms of holding the demand generation team accountable," shared Alex Turner, Director of Sales Development at Wrike. "As long as that prospect still works at the company and we can sell to them, SDRs shouldn't be rejecting leads."

As with most things in life, coffee helps to illuminate this point. If a coworker brings you a large coffee, you might not finish it before it cools. You can return to it at a later point for a quick reheating: *recycle*. (Note: only litterbugs and people who stow their jackets in airplane overhead bins drink room temperature coffee). Now, if the first sip causes a spit-take, you aren't likely to return to that cup. Best to throw it away, never to be discussed again: *reject*.

Marketing tends to be cautious about the *reject* versus *recycle* distinction. Often, rejected leads are removed from the count of MQLs passed to sales development, requiring a replacement to achieve their quota. To give all parties a warm fuzzy feeling, you can create a validation rule to prevent records that are in "Working" status from being rejected.

Your formula might look like:

```
$UserRole.Name = "Sales_Development_Rep" &&
ISPICKVAL(Status, "Rejected") &&
NOT(ISPICKVAL(PRIORVALUE(Status), "MQL"))
```

Should an SDR attempt to reject a prospect after one or two attempts, they'll trip the validation rule (see figure 9.3).

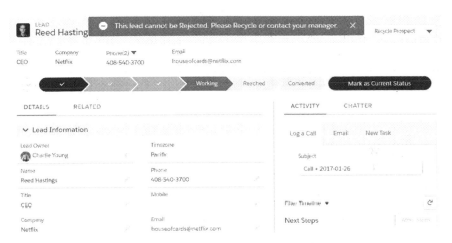

Figure 9.3 – Rejection validation rule

On occasion, I've seen companies require reps to supply a rejection reason. But since you've set hard-and-fast rules about when "Rejected" can be used, you can skip this step. A prospect can only be rejected when they aren't a *real prospect*. No other reason or explanation is required. With "Recycled" however, additional details are needed. A prospect can be recycled for any number of reasons—they were never reached, they have no budget, they just purchased a competitor, and so on. A **Recycle Reason** field gives marketing real value, as SDRs aren't saying this prospect will *never buy*, just that they won't *buy now*.

You can create a custom picklist field and use a validation rule to require a reason when status is set to "Recycled." You'll likely add additional options to meet your company's needs, but common recycle reasons include:

▶ No contact (set as the default option)

▶ No immediate interest/need

▶ Using Competitor A

"Recycle or nurture reason is a key field for us," Vanessa Porter, Director of Marketing at SnapApp, told me. "We use it in marketing automation as we determine how to continue marketing to that prospect. Whether an SDR had a conversation with a prospect and they're just researching, or if they were using a competitor, or even if they never responded to SDR outreach, we use that information to make sure we're placing them in proper nurture streams."

Marketers like Vanessa rely on this intelligence to market to and (hopefully) requalify prospects. Your goal should be to deliver the data marketing needs while also making it easy for SDRs to close the loop. The overwhelming majority of recycled prospects will be ones who didn't respond to SDR outreach.

You can build a quick, two-click process for these "No contact" prospects. First, create a record update action called "Recycle Prospect" and add it to the *Salesforce1 and Lightning Experience Actions* section of the page layout. Add the **Lead Status** and **Recycle Reason** fields and default the values to "Recycled" and "No contact." Next, create a workflow rule to reassign to a marketing queue/user when the **Lead Status** is changed to "Recycle." This process both prompts reps to provide a reason for recycle and clears the deadwood from their views once they do. Figure 9.4 below is what an SDR sees after pressing the [Recycle Prospect] button.

Figure 9.4 – Recycle prospect experience

Label Contacts with a Status

If you opt to have SDRs work from *Accounts & Contacts*, you should replicate **Lead Status** on *Contacts*. You can create a **Contact Status** picklist field. You can keep consistency between *Leads* and *Contacts* by using the same six statuses mentioned earlier in this chapter. You should also consider using an **Account Status** picklist field on *Accounts* as well. After all, wouldn't it be helpful to extend your funnel and know how many accounts are being actively prospected?

Pete Gracey, CEO at QuotaFactory, shared his thinking with me. "You want to net out where an account stands on a spectrum from *prospect* to *customer*. Everyone, from your CEO to the newest support rep should be able to look at this field and know an account's relationship with your company. In a perfect world, all of this would be automated and you'd eliminate the ability for reps to misclassify accounts."

Let's pick up Pete's challenge of automating **Account Status**. As a first step, we need to define our options. You'll likely want to customize this language, but here's a starting point:

▶ **Target**- a prospect account you haven't attempted to reach

▶ **Cold**- a prospect account that hasn't responded to outreach

▶ **Working**- an account where 1+ people are being prospected

▶ **Selling**- an account with an active selling opportunity

▶ **Win-back**- a recent sales loss, cancellation, or non-renewal

▶ **Customer**- an account with a recent sales win

In a single buyer scenario, it is easy enough to use Process Builder or workflow rules to update **Account Status** when a **Contact Status** changes. But what happens when multiple buyers are being prospected at the same time? How do you aggregate and update the account with the most advanced status?

To accomplish this, you can again turn to Process Builder and Visual Workflow to do the heavy lifting. From the *Opportunity* object, a simple Process Builder can update the related *Account* record. From the *Contact* object, an auto-launched flow is required. At a high-level, every time a **Contact Status** changes, you'll use flow to iterate through all *Contacts* related to the

Account. You'll build logic into the Flow to determine the most appropriate **Account Status**. Your logic might resemble figure 9.5 below:

IF	THEN
A contact's status changes to "Recycled" and there are no other contacts in "Working" or "Reached"	Cold
A contact's status changes to "Working" and **Account Status** isn't "Selling" or "Customer"	Working
Any contact's status changes to "Qualified"	Selling
An open opportunity is created	Selling
An open opportunity is won	Customer
A renewal opportunity is lost	Win-back

Figure 9.5 – Account status logic

This list should get you started. I recommend you white board out all the paths for when a change on either a *Contact* or an *Opportunity* should update the **Account Status**. Your goal is to create a meaningful and reliable indicator of each account's relationship with your company. Rather than relying on SDR, Account Executives, or Customer Success to update the field, you can leave it to automation.

CHAPTER 10

⚡

MAKE CAMPAIGNS MEANINGFUL

IN A BRAND-NEW INSTANCE of Salesforce, you'll find just five options for the **Lead Source** field. I've been in mature orgs that presented a small army of choices. I once worked on a project to bring the number of lead sources down from over two hundred. Marketing went kicking and screaming the whole way to the final list of thirty-eight options before we declared victory and moved on.

The moral of the story is that people are touchy about lead sources.

But for all the drama, SDRs rarely pay the field much attention. *Display*, *PPC*, and *Website* read exactly the same way to reps: this is inbound. Unless they are compensated differently based on "marketing-sourced" or "self-generated," I don't advise even exposing the field to your reps. SDRs care a great deal, on the other hand, about a prospect's campaign history. A prospect who registered for a webinar is one thing. A prospect who attended a tradeshow, stopped by the booth, and then registered for that same webinar is another entirely. There is real value in campaign history. But too often this opportunity is missed.

The first mistake I see occurs with naming campaigns. Believe it or not, AMER--Web--3ʳᵈ-Party-Site--Topic-A--Organic--FY16Q2 isn't super helpful for a rep trying to orient themselves with a prospect's campaign narrative.

I completely understand why marketing might need a complex, and lengthy, campaign name. You should create a custom **Marketing Name** field for their tracking needs. The SDR-facing campaign name should be *in human*. "Formula & Analytics Webinar with Steve Molis" is a human-centric

61

campaign name. Making that change alone is a huge step forward.

Beyond campaign names, you should create meaningful campaign member statuses. The default **Campaign Member Status** values do little to explain what actions a prospect took. In the context of the Steve Molis webinar mentioned above, are you instantly clear on what *Planned, Sent,* and *Responded* statuses mean? Wouldn't *Invited, RSVP'd, Attended,* and *Active in Q&A* be more meaningful?

These little details will help your SDRs immensely—in both their messaging and during live conversations with prospects. There is little worse than saying "I see you attended our webinar" to a prospect who didn't. Sounding like a moron, it turns out, does little to boost credibility.

Beyond names and statuses, you can serve your reps by turning a *Campaign* record into a "marketing asset package." Morgan J. Ingram is an Account-Based Marketing Specialist at Terminus and host of *The SDR Chronicles* on YouTube. "When marketing publishes a new ebook, sales needs the CliffsNotes®," he commented. "Ideally every SDR would read every piece of content that's being produced. But realistically, that isn't going to happen. SDRs need an executive summary, some talking points, and sample emails, voicemails, and call openings to get going."

Morgan makes a great point. Think about how many pieces of content your company produced over the last few quarters. Are you sure that your CMO could hit the highlights of each and every one? Is it fair to assume more from an SDR? Turning a *Campaign* record into a "marketing asset package" doesn't require a ton of effort. At the most basic level, a rep needs:

- ▶ A link to the PDF/recording itself
- ▶ The elevator pitch, key takeaways, a list of logical follow-up questions
- ▶ (Optional) A link to a Google Doc with sample voicemails, emails, tweets, etc.

You can edit the *Campaign* Compact Layout to make these fields accessible when hovering over a **Campaign Name** (figure 10.1 below). This gives your reps access to key context that will help them have intelligent and productive sales conversations.

Figure 10.1 – Campaign compact layout

Say a prospect had stopped into your party at a tradeshow. The next day, they attended your CEO's session and met her afterwards. A few weeks later, they registered for an upcoming webinar. Putting all those actions together might look something like figure 10.2 below.

Figure 10.2 – Meaningful campaign history

That is a world away from what most reps encounter when scanning campaign history today. Using meaningful language and providing additional context is how we in sales operations enable our users. Take these steps and your campaign histories will build better conversations, not baffle with internal jargon.

CHAPTER 11

⚡

LEVERAGE LINKEDIN AND LOCATION

THE FINAL TWO of the pre-call 4Ls are LinkedIn and Location. A long time ago in a galaxy far away, reps could see their prospects' LinkedIn information from within Salesforce. This was back when LinkedIn played nicely with other CRMs and well before the acquisition by Microsoft. Although that *kumbaya* moment has passed, you should still make it as easy as possible for reps to jump from Salesforce to LinkedIn.

LinkedIn can be a gold mine for driving personalized and effective sales conversations. Jamie Shanks, author of *Social Selling Mastery*, shared, "An SDR's job is to reduce the ROE (Return-on-Effort) to drive new conversations forward. Linking LinkedIn and Salesforce gives reps quick access to the language a prospect uses, what they find important, and how they measure themselves. It also presents their relationships to your customer base and gives a roadmap to their 'sphere of influence' and the other buyers in the buying committee."

As Jamie pointed out, there's tremendous value available to your SDRs on LinkedIn. To save reps from tedious LinkedIn sleuthing, you can add a **LinkedIn URL** field. Once a rep finds a prospect on LinkedIn they can paste the profile URL on the record itself. Then it's never more than a click away. This works exceptionally well the second, third, and fourth time a rep wants to scan a prospect's LinkedIn profile. But finding a prospect's profile that first time requires a fair bit of copying, pasting, and toggling between Salesforce and the LinkedIn search bar.

You can save your reps the hassle with a simple workflow rule. Any time a new lead is qualified (aka when **Lead Status** is set to "MQL" for example) and the field is currently blank, you can prefill the **LinkedIn URL** with this formula.

```
"http://www.linkedin.com/vsearch/p?firstName=" &
FirstName & "&lastName=" & LastName &
"&company=" & Company & "&openAdvancedForm=true"
```

Now, when a rep first lands on a new prospect, they encounter figure 11.1 below:

Figure 11.1 – LinkedIn URL

They would then click through, find Mike's LinkedIn URL, paste it in the **LinkedIn URL** field (*just once*) and voila! When they want to visit Mike's record subsequently, his LinkedIn page is only a click away.

Joes in Different Area Codes

You might be surprised to see location as the final of the pre-call research 4Ls. In my interviews with SDRs, I wasn't expecting it to come up quite so often. But, as they explained it to me, time zones are critical for planning their days for maximum productivity.

Depending on the research you cite, the best times to call and connect with a prospect are either "before 9AM and after 4PM," "after 6PM," or "between 10AM and 4PM." Isn't that helpful! The only thing these studies seem to agree on is that they can't *all* be right. To maximize your SDRs chances of success, you need to answer two questions:

1. How do SDRs know which time zone a given prospect is in?
2. How does your sales development team know the best times to reach *your* specific prospects?

Let's take these in order.

From friend to friend and mentor to mentee a fabulous time zone formula has been passed around the Salesforce admin-sphere. While US-centric, it can be adapted to meet the needs of just about any organization. There are more than five-hundred area codes in the United States. As you might expect, this **Timezone** field's formula is lengthy.

```
IF( ISBLANK( Phone ),NULL, if( CONTAINS(
"206:209:213:253:310:323:360:408:415:425:503:509:510:530:559:562:604:619:626:650:66
1:702:707:714:760:775:778:805:818:831:858:867:909:916:925:949:951:971:424:442:541:6
57", LEFT( SUBSTITUTE( Phone, "(", ""),3)),"Pacific",

IF( CONTAINS( "208:250:303:307:385:403:406:435:480:505:520:602:623:
719:720:780:801:928:970:575", LEFT( SUBSTITUTE( Phone, "(", ""),3)),"Mountain", if(
CONTAINS("204:205:210:214:217:218:224:
225:228:251:254:256:262:270:281:306:308:309:312:314:316:318:319:320:325:334:337:361
:402:405: 409:414:417:430:432:469:479:501:504:
507:512:515:563:573:580:601:605:608:612:615:618:620:630:636:641:651:660:662:682:708
: 712:713:715:731:763:769:773:785:806:815:
816:817:830:832:847:901:903:913:915:918:920:931:936:940:952:956:972:979:985:331:870
", LEFT( SUBSTITUTE( Phone, "(", ""),3)),"Central",

IF( CONTAINS("201:202:203:207:212:215:216:219:226:229:231:234:
239:240:248:252:267:269:276:289:301:302:304:305:313:315:321:330:336:
339:345:347:351:352:386:404:407:410:412:416:418:419:434:438:440:443:450:470:475:478
:484:502:508:513:514:516:517:518:519:551:561:567: 570:571:
540:585:586:603:606:607:609:610:613:614:616:617:631:646:
647:649:678:703:704:705:706:716:717:718:724:727:732:734:740:754:757:
770:772:774:781:786:802:803:804:810:813:814:819:828:835:843:845:848:
856:857:859:860:862:863:864:865:876:878:904:905:908:910:912:914:917:
919:937:941:947:954:959:973:978:980:260:272:317:401:413:423:574:765: 812:989",
LEFT( SUBSTITUTE( Phone, "(", ""),3)),"Eastern",
```

```
IF( CONTAINS("800:877:856:866:844:888",LEFT( SUBSTITUTE(Phone, "(",""),3)),"Toll
Free",

IF( CONTAINS("850:906",LEFT( SUBSTITUTE(Phone,"(",""),3)),"E or C",

IF( CONTAINS("701",LEFT( SUBSTITUTE(Phone,"(",""),3)),"C or M",

IF( CONTAINS("907:808",LEFT( SUBSTITUTE(Phone,"(",""),3)),"Their Own!", "Notify Ad-
min" )))))))))
```

Now that is a thing of beauty. Thanks to more admins than I can list, that formula has been honed and tweaked to return "Eastern" for 212 in New York City, "Pacific" for 415 in San Francisco, and "Notify Admin" if all else fails. You can find a copy-and-paste-able version of this formula here: http://sdrbook.io/timezonesfdc (all lowercase).

From a list view, reps can sort by time zone to prioritize (see figure 11.2 below). They can plan their calling by focusing on the time zone with the highest likelihood of making a live connect at any given moment.

LEADS
Today's Leads ▼

NAME	COMPANY ↑	LEAD STAT...	PHONE	TIMEZONE
Phyllis Cotton	3CLogic	MQL	(504) 757-1000	Central
Althea Murphy	A Foundation	MQL	(303) 555-1212	Mountain
Arnal Ross	Amet Corporati...	MQL	(617) 555-1212	Eastern
Lauren Unswo...	Bessemer Vent...	MQL	(617) 588-1700	Eastern
Bertha Boyer	Farmara Coop. ...	MQL	(813) 644-4200	Eastern
Joshua Adragna	Mattermark	MQL	(415) 367-4567	Pacific
Mike Braund	Metropolitan H...	MQL	(410) 381 2334	Eastern
Leah Blevins	Nec Ante Ltd	MQL	(303) 555-1212	Mountain
Pub Lisher	New York Times	MQL	212 556-7777	Eastern
Florence Sims	Pellentesque As..	MQL	(503) 555-1212	Pacific

Figure 11.2 – Time zones in list views

Now, let's turn to the second question: *how does your sales development team know the best times to reach your specific prospects?* This is the kind of intelligence that organizations build up over time. But to harness it, you need to build the underlying infrastructure.

Reporting on Connect Rate by Hour

Figure 11.3 is where you want to end up.

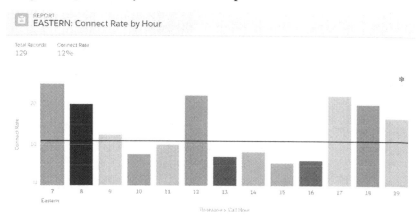

Figure 11.3 – Connect rate reporting

This tells the story visually. For prospects in the eastern time zone, *early*, *lunch*, and *late* are the best times to connect by phone. Mid-morning and mid-afternoon are the worst. To get to this report, you need both a **Timezone** field (on *Leads* and *Contacts*) and **Call Hour** custom field on *Tasks*.

The **Call Hour** field extracts the hour in which the *Task* was created. Seems simple enough, right? But to complicate matters, you need to differentiate a real "sales touch" from a marketing automation, email logging, or other system-generated one. For example, if an SDR sends an email to Pauline Prospect. There will be a Salesforce task for that. If Pauline opens the email, another task. If she clicks a link, yet another. And then if she submits a form on your website, there's one more! On and on. Including these records only serves to skew your "Connect Rate by Hour" report.

To handle this, you should build logic into your **Call Hour** field's formula. One way to do this is to rely on a custom **Disposition** field (discussed in more detail in chapter 13). For now, all that matters is that for "real" dials, this field will never be blank. For marketing automation, form submissions, and other system-generated *Tasks*, it will be blank. Your **Call Hour** formula would be:

```
IF(
  ISBLANK( TEXT(Disposition__c)),
  NULL,
  VALUE( MID( TEXT( CreatedDate), 12, 2 ) ) ) - 4 )
```

So for a call logged at 8:32 AM, the **Call Hour** would be 8. For a call logged at 6:05 PM, the **Call Hour** would be 18. And so on. This gives you the x-axis in the report above. Just make sure to filter your report to exclude records with a blank **Call Hour**. Alternately, you could filter your report to exclude these *Tasks* by subject. But this can get complicated and tends to slow down running your reports.

With your "Connect Rate by Hour" report, you can slice and dice by title, industry, time zone, etc. Since your SDRs are logging calls to satisfy management reporting requirements, why not return some value to them and help them better plan their days? I call this the power of *medium-sized data*.

Morgan Ingram, the SDR and YouTube host mentioned in the last chapter, put it to me this way. "If you don't schedule your life, your life will schedule you. First thing every morning, I want to be calling people and trying to catch them early. It matters when it's early where they are. I save LinkedIn, Twitter, and email for times when prospects are likely to be in meetings."

When an SDR comes in first thing in the morning and faces fifteen new leads, the **Timezone** field is their best friend. For an SDR with prospects across the United States, a model "perfect morning" might resemble figure 11.4:

TIME	ACTION
7-8AM	Call Eastern time zone
8-9AM	Call Eastern & Central
9-10AM	Call Central & Mountain
10-11AM	Call Mountain & Pacific
11-12PM	Call Pacific & Eastern

Figure 11.4 – A perfect SDR morning

You can't support that kind of workstream without the data. And that's exactly what the **Timezone** and **Call Hour** fields, combined with the "Connect Rate by Hour" report, deliver.

Note All the Numbers

Consider the humble phone number.

Out of the box, Salesforce gives us quite a few phone number fields. On *Accounts*, we have **Phone**. On *Contacts*, we have **Phone**, **Assistant Phone**, **Home Phone**, **Mobile Phone**, and **Other Phone**. When a rep is trying to reach a prospect, there is a hierarchy of phone number usefulness. They rank, from best to worst:

▶ Mobile phone (the one to rule them all)

▶ Direct dial (golden ticket)

▶ Assistant phone (lukewarm coffee)

▶ Main company switchboard (7th circle of hell)

To give your reps the best chance of making contact, I suggest adding one more formula field on *Contacts*—**Account Phone**. As you might have guessed, this formula brings the phone number from the main company record down to the contact level. When a new prospect is imported, say from Data.com or a web form, it's helpful to compare the phone number that has been supplied with the main company switchboard, side by side.

You can coach your reps to use the standard **Phone** field to hold direct dial phone numbers only. This is extremely useful when your reps are executing "power hours" (focused calling blitzes) to gain a few extra live connects. It gums up the works massively when every third phone number is a switchboard instead of a direct dial. You can add these fields to page layout as illustrated in figure 11.5 below:

Figure 11.5 – Triple phone fields

A quick word on calling a prospect's mobile phone. Not too long ago only the boldest SDRs would dare call a prospect on their mobile. But times, and attitudes, are changing. I asked my friend Steve Richard, Chief Revenue Officer at ExecVision, for his thoughts. "As long as an SDR has a good reason to call and has done their homework, most prospects won't object. If they get upset, reps can respond 'This is the number I found for you. My apologies. Would it be better if I called you back on a different number another time?' Politely backing off causes most prospects to lean in and agree to a short, unplanned conversation."

Using a mobile number is entirely appropriate when a) it has been shared by the prospect or b) it's included in their email signature. Once a rep books a meeting, asking for the prospect's mobile number should be part of their process. The single best way to confirm an upcoming meeting is with a text message. Everyone—from the ten-year-old next door to the CEO on the cover of *Fortune*—reaches for their phone when a text comes in.

CHAPTER 12

⚡

CREATE COMPELLING CONVERSATIONS

"EVERY COMPANY has three or four pieces of information that are foundational from a sales and marketing perspective," Phill Keene, Manager of Demand Generation at Octiv, shared with me. "These are the key segmentation and qualification points that drive SDR messaging, meeting criteria, and nurture marketing. It might be location, industry, and size of company. Or maybe functional area, technologies in use, and number of sales reps. Each company needs to identify their key fields and make sure they're gathered."

I like Phill's *rule of three*. There's a fine balance between SDR conversations driving account intelligence and SDRs being data analysts and prospect interrogators. There is a strong temptation to ask SDRs to collect "just one more data point" whenever they talk to a prospect. The problem is, over time these *just ones* add up. You can use three data points as a baseline. Four is fine. Five is borderline. And six is a *doubling*. Beyond that and your SDRs aren't prospecting for opportunity, they're conducting phone surveys for the Pew Research Center.

When an SDR does learn one or more of those pieces of information, it can have major downstream benefits. They can better customize subsequent messages. If they do set a meeting for an account executive, these fields can be pulled into a "New Meeting Brief" email template. If they don't qualify the prospect, marketing can customize nurture tracks based on what has been learned to date.

Joy Shutters-Helbing is a Salesforce Administrator at VISANOW. I asked her how she thinks through this balance. "The smaller you are, the easier it is

72

to review the text history to get the picture. The bigger you are, the more you rely on data and reports. But no company plans to stay small forever. These types of data are what's going to drive decision making for the business. But if reps don't understand what's in it for them and it's a pain to populate, they just won't do it."

The best way to formalize this practice is to create fields in Salesforce. As Joy mentioned, open text fields make it easier to skim and comprehend a prospect's story, but they're terrible for reporting and marketing segmentation. Without constraints, it is easy to go overboard copying-and-pasting into text fields. Pretty soon, reps have compiled a novella on a given prospect. Then when they do make a live connect, skimming that wall of words to find the salient details is impossible. On the other hand, picklist fields are great for reporting. But they can be limiting. You want your reps to gather enough information to feel, be, and act prepared. While also giving the rest of the organization data that is actionable. Marketing, for instance, needs to be able to report on prospects using *Competitor A* without reading hundreds or thousands of open text notes.

That is where the sweet spot lies.

A mostly picklists, rarely open text approach is often best. This balances the needs of the broader stakeholders while still presenting information so that reps can actually work it into their messaging on the fly.

Let's turn to an example to illustrate the point.

Logging Pre-Call Research

Imagine you work for a company that offers conference room display and scheduling software. You know, the cool iPad displays that are mounted outside meeting rooms and seek to solve double-booking, room hoarding, and the like. In this example, the *key fields* your organization cares about might be:

▶ Which calendar system a prospect is using

▶ How many conference rooms they have

▶ Their primary pain point

73

► Who is leading the project (Office Admin/IT/Sales/etc.)

You can create an "SDR Qualification section" on your page layout to house these details. In addition to the fields mentioned above, you might add a **SDR Notes** long text area to capture additional points of pre-call research (see figure 12.1).

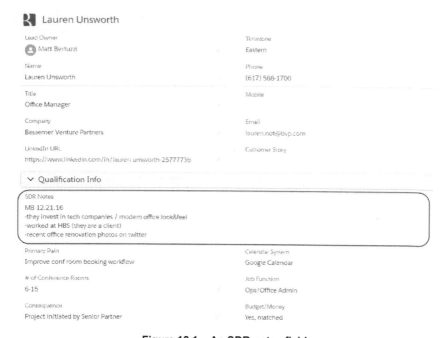

Figure 12.1 – An SDR notes field

Those are the types of research notes (and bullet points) that SDRs can weave into their messages and conversations. "In 10 years as a sales trainer, I saw sales reps spending so much time 'doing research'," shared ExecVision CEO Steve Richard. "Then they'd get into a conversation and wouldn't reference any of it. Having studied what works and what doesn't, I can tell you that reps are 70% more likely to book a meeting if they tell the prospect about the research they did."

Our job in sales ops is to build a framework for turning pre-call research into during-call *telling*. That's exactly what a "mostly picklists, rarely open text" approach delivers.

Leveraging Pre-Call Research

I was working with a client recently who wanted to do something interesting. Their marketing director had come back from Dreamforce feeling inspired. She wanted to house customer stories inside Salesforce and explained her thinking, "My team is writing up all these fantastic customer stories for our website, for our collateral, and for our lead nurturing. We've always just told the sales team, 'Hey, we have a great new story up. Go check it out.' But we've never put them at reps' fingertips."

Her goal was not only get these stories into Salesforce, but to also make it easy for reps to put them into use. To accomplish this, we built a *Customer Story* custom object (figure 12.2). The key fields included the qualification information described above as well as:

▶ A visual, image formula field for **OK to Reference**

▶ A link to the full story's URL

▶ The executive summary of the story itself

Figure 12.2 – The customer story custom object

This solved the first challenge of getting these stories centralized into Salesforce. But the second goal, making them accessible as part of an SDR's daily workflow required something more. The marketing director shared, "From our web forms and from their pre-call research, we already have a good deal of information on a prospect. In a perfect world, reps could just click a button and find all the relevant stories."

Thankfully, you can accomplish exactly this—without any custom code— by embedding a Flow into the record page. Your flow (figure 12.3 below) does all the heavy lifting of searching for the best matched customer stories based on the qualification information fields on the prospect record.

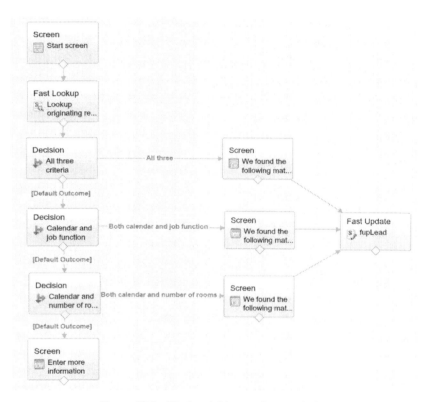

Figure 12.3 – Find matching customer stories

Figure 12.4 shows the flow embedded in the page layout.

Say this prospect uses Google Calendar, has 16-30 meeting rooms, and is within the IT function. When an SDR clicks "Next" in the *Search Customer Stories* component, they are presented with the following matched stories sorted with the most recently modified at the top (figure 12.5).

Figure 12.4 – Embedded custom story flow

Figure 12.5 – Matched customer stories

An SDR can choose whichever story they want to link and click "Next" to update the prospect's record. Then, they can hover over that field to find the details and a link to the story's PDF (figure 12.6).

Figure 12.6 – A linked customer story

There are other—and likely more elegant—ways to solve this business need. But this gives you one example of the power of turning required fields from a negative to positive. Surfacing relevant customer stories is an "all carrot/no stick" approach to driving adoption for qualification information fields.

Up to this point, we've worked hard to simplify an SDR's process for identifying and planning their prospect outreach. In Part 3, we'll turn our attention to supporting them as they make contact.

PART 3

CONTACT

A map is very helpful for getting around Paris. But not if the map you're using is a map of New York.

—RUSS ROBERTS (quoting Nassim Taleb)

CHAPTER 13

⚡

LEVERAGE PATH

AMYRA RAND KNOWS scaling sales at high-growth companies. Amyra is the VP of Sales at Criteria Corp. and shared her perspective on SDR outreach with me. "There's a science to sales development. It's in how many times you touch a prospect, how frequently you make attempts, and which message you go out with. Once you talk to a prospect, that's when the art begins. That's when each rep, as a savvy sales person, has to know which questions to ask and how to lead them down a path. But up until that point, it's the formula. I don't want my reps having to think about that piece. I need something that enables that rigor and that science."

Over the next few chapters, we'll turn our attention to optimizing how reps make contact. We'll look at tactics and approaches to enable Amyra's "rigor and science" within Salesforce. In Chapter 0, we briefly touched on Path—the visual status/stage management component for Salesforce1 and the Lightning Experience. Salesforce describes Path as giving:

> *[Y]our sales team the guidance they need to close their deals with fewer delays—from anywhere. When you set up sales paths, you determine which fields are key for your sales reps to complete. You'll also provide tips, potential gotchas, and even words of encouragement to keep sales reps eager to close their deals faster.*

At the time of this writing, Path is available on *Leads*, *Opportunities*, *Quotes*, and custom objects. My hope is that it is extended to *Accounts & Contacts* in short order. This will be a key element for those companies implementing "account-based" sales and marketing strategies. Beyond Path's distance-to-goal visual, there is huge value in the ability to highlight specific fields (per status) and offer guidance with text, images, or links.

To review, our **Contact Status** and/or **Lead Status** options include:

- ▶ Rejected
- ▶ Recycled
- ▶ MQL
- ▶ Working
- ▶ Reached
- ▶ Qualified

In chapter 8, we created a [Recycle Prospect] button to prompt reps to provide a **Recycle Reason**. Alternatively, we could have used Path. Clicking on the "Recycled" status brings up the key fields for this stage and customizable text guidance (figure 13.1):

Figure 13.1 – Path for recycling prospects

Here, your reps can set the status to "Recycle," choose a reason from the picklist, and [Mark as Current Status]. Similarly, for the "MQL" status, we can surface key fields like **Best Matched Account** and a few of the 4Ls fields like **Timezone**, **Last Campaign** and **LinkedIn URL** (figure 13.2):

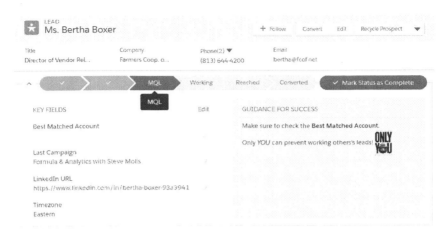

Figure 13.2 – Path for MQL status

You can choose the fields and add the guidance most appropriate for your team. Text, bullets, images, and hyperlinks are all supported. You might show an image for a certain stage, link out to process documentation for another, and share bulleted reminders for a third. To get you started, "Key Field" and "Guidance" recommendations are presented in figure 13.3.

STATUS	FIELDS	GUIDANCE
Rejected	None	The SLA for rejection
Recycled	Lead Status, Recycle Reason	A reminder to supply a reason for recycle
MQL	Best Matched Account, Last Campaign, LinkedIn URL, Time zone	Reminder of outreach cadence and image of the process
Working	Time zone, Last Attempt Date, # of Attempts	Link to *Cadence SLA* Google Doc and image of the process
Reached	Your key qualification fields	Link to *Qualification Criteria* Google Doc

Figure 13.3 – Path recommendations

Automate Your Lead Statuses

Reps, it turns out, don't enjoy managing lead statuses. At best, updating a status requires an extra click or two. And at worst, forgetting to change

"MQL" to "Working" makes it appear they're slacking on prospect follow-up. Here's a simple, if a tad radical, suggestion: *automate lead statuses*. Well, to be more accurate, automate when a prospect should move from "MQL" to "Working" and from "Working" to "Reached."

Salesforce MVP and Salesforce Operations Manager, Kristi Guzman, shared this story with me. "Here at MapAnything, we were facing a problem that's pretty common. Our reps were working leads and logging calls, but forgetting to update the lead statuses. This skewed the numbers and made it appear that we had an artificially high number of uncontacted leads. In the moment, changing the lead status adds no value to the reps. But it is critical for the business and our data integrity."

Like any seasoned Salesforce admin, Kristi turned to the community for suggestions using the #askforce hashtag (figure 13.4):

Kristi Guzman
@KristiForce

Can I have logged activity update a Lead Status somehow (Flow? DLRS?) or is WhoID a special snowflake (aka bane of my existence) #askforce

11.31 AM - 21 Jun 2016

Figure 13.4 – Tweet from @KristiForce

Nerd-level specifics warning(!) as the next paragraph delves into some gory details.

As you may know, a Salesforce *Task*'s **Name** field can relate to either a *Contact* or a *Lead*. This makes life easy for users and hellacious for admins trying to update records using automation. Traditional workflow rules won't work here since the relationship is polymorphic and not deterministic. Now, polymorphic is just database-speak for #WhySalesforceAdminsDrink. In short, it means that the **WhoId** field can relate either a *Contact* or a *Lead* to a given task. Next time you're stuck talking to someone you'd rather not be, bring this subject up. It's a fantastic conversation ender. *That reminds me of the nature of using polymorphic keys in database design*. I guarantee they'll excuse themselves.

Okay, back to Kristi.

Doug Ayers, an 8x Salesforce Certified Senior Developer at GearsCRM, saw Kristi's tweet and answered the call. On his blog (https://douglascayers.com), he wrote:

We're able to create custom Contact and Lead lookup fields on the Task object and use Process Builder to populate them appropriately based on the value of the WhoId. Then we will have deterministic lookup fields that Workflow Rules or Process Builder can reference.

Believe me when I say, those forty-five words are a game changer. We'll return to Doug's solution in the next chapter. But before we do, we need to discuss several fields that are central to activity reporting. In the rest of this book, I will refer to the following fields:

1. **Disposition**- an *Activity* custom field that reflects the outcome of a given call. You can customize this to the terminology your organization uses. But I tend to stick with these:

    -   VM: left a voicemail
    -   No Result: a live conversation that didn't move the sales process forward
    -   Referral: a live conversation when the SDR was referred to another party
    -   Next Step: a live conversation that *did* move the sales process forward
    -   Ghost: a call where a voicemail was *not* left
    -   Email: email sent

2. **IsConnect**- an *Activity* custom checkbox formula field. The formula references the **Disposition** field to return TRUE for a live phone conversation (i.e., No Result, Referral, Next Step) and FALSE for everything else. This field is particularly important in connect and connect rate reporting.

3. **Last Attempt Date**- a *Lead* or *Contact* custom date field. You might ask, why not use the standard **Last Activity Date** field? Well, because it is too easily polluted. Email syncing and marketing automation systems are constantly logging form submissions, email opens, and links being clicked. Each of these creates a new task and updates the last activity. This makes it difficult for an SDR to

quickly orient to when the last *human* activity took place. This is a key field for building cadences, which we'll discuss shortly.

4. **Last Connect Date**- another *Lead* or *Contact* custom date field. Like the field above, you'll use this to track the date of the most recent *human* activity that resulted in a live phone conversation.

5. **# of Attempts**- a *Lead* or *Contact* custom number field for tracking the number of attempts made by an SDR. This field is particularly important in meeting and reporting on lead follow-up Service Level Agreements (SLAs).

These five fields are invaluable for SDR leadership to effectively evaluate and coach reps. And as you'll see in the next chapter, we can use advanced automation to populate them all.

CHAPTER 14

✦

BUILD YOUR ACTIVITY PROCESS

OKAY. Let's return to Doug Ayers and his custom lookup and Process Builder solution.

It's hard to believe, but Process Builder was only released in 2015. Prior to that, attempting to solve this particular need would have required custom code. Now we can handle it entirely declaratively. Button click admins, unite!

I've adapted Doug's solution to populate the custom fields mentioned in the previous chapter. But the credit for inspiring me—and hitting upon the use of lookup fields—one hundred percent belongs to Doug.

To build this automation, you'll create a Process Builder on *Tasks* similar to what you see in figure 14.1 below:

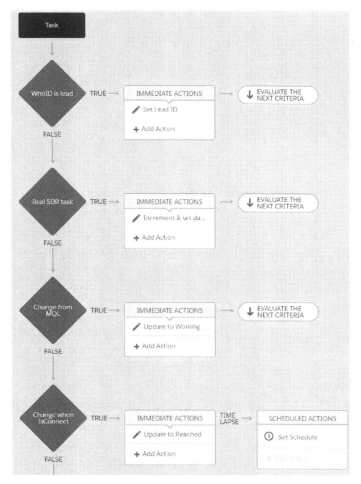

Figure 14.1 – Process on *Tasks*

This Process has four nodes and utilizes "Evaluate the Next Criteria" to run through them in order. Figure 14.2 shares a brief summary of how it operates:

NODE	CRITERIA	ACTIONS
1	For any *Task* that is a) associated with a *Lead* b) completed, and c) not system generated	Fill the **Lead** lookup

2	For any *Task* with the **Lead** lookup filled	Set the **Last Attempt Date** field. Increment the **# of Attempts**. And if applicable, set the **Last Connect Date**.
3	For any *Task* with the **Lead** lookup filled and where the *Lead* is in "MQL" status	Change the **Lead Status** to "Working"
4	For any *Task* with the **Lead** lookup filled and where **IsConnect** is TRUE	Change the **Lead Status** to "Reached"

Figure 14.2 – Summary of *Task* process

Notice that several of the nodes might fire for a single activity.

For example, if an SDR called a brand new "MQL" and had a live conversation, three nodes would be true. The Process would update the **Lead** lookup field on the *Task* (#1), it would set the **Last Attempt Date** to today, increment the **# of Attempts** to one, and set the **Last Connect Date** to today (#2), and finally it would change the **Lead Status** to "Reached" (#3). I remember working with a company just a few years ago that required reps to log all these fields manually. This one process would have saved them up to seven clicks per task! That is improving user experience through automation.

Note: if your SDRs are working *Accounts & Contacts*, you'll want to configure Process Builder to handle a **Contact** lookup field as well as **Contact Status**.

Supercharge Your Reporting

At this point, you might object that all this seems a fair bit of work. And it is . . . for the admin.

But we're trying to balance two contradictory forces. On the one hand, you're saving SDRs from having to click-click-click-log "all of the things." On the other, you're meeting the need for SDR managers to have reliable data for coaching and leading their teams. Let me give you a few examples of reporting that this automation allows.

First, recall the "Connect Rate by Hour" reporting we covered in chapter 10. That report isn't possible without your **Disposition** and **IsConnect** fields. Or say you wanted to report on the Service Level Agreements (SLAs) between marketing and the SDRs. You might have an SLA that states:

▶ "MQL" prospects must have at least one attempt within one day

▶ "Working" prospects must have a recent attempt within one month

▶ "Reached" prospects must have a recent connect within one quarter

To report on this, you can create a formula to track SLA compliance based on our custom fields. Your **Missed SLA?** field's formula would be:

```
IF(
   (ISPICKVAL(Status, "MQL") && of_Attempts__c < 1) ||
   (ISPICKVAL(Status, "Working") &&
   Last_Attempt_Date__c + 30 <  today()) ||
   (ISPICKVAL(Status, "Reached") &&
   Last_Connect_Date__c + 90 <  today()),
   TRUE,
   FALSE
   )
```

This formula will return a checked box—meaning the SLA has been missed—as specified in the table below (figure 14.3).

LEAD STATUS	SLA TERMS
MQL	**# of Attempts** is greater or equal to 1
Working	**Last Attempt Date** within the last *30 days*.
Reached	**Last Connect Date** within the last *90 days*.

Figure 14.3 – Marketing SDR SLA

You can use this field to report on prospects by owner, by source, or by last campaign and see how many are outside the SLA window.

In the example below (figure 14.4), seven of ten records are outside their SLA—including three which are still in "MQL" status. Rather than a manager having to dig into *Leads* and *Tasks* to confirm what might have fallen through the cracks, SDR leaders can trust in Salesforce data and highlight specific records for their reps to act on.

Total Records	Total Missed SLA?
10	8

LAST NAME	COMPANY / ACCOUNT	LEAD STATUS ↑	# OF ATTEMPTS	LAST ATTEMPT DATE	MISSED SLA?
Feager	International Shipping Co.	MQL	.	.	✓
Hull	Dictum Cursus Ltd	MQL	.	.	✓
Fleming	Dolor Institute	MQL	.	.	✓
Ford	Id Enim Institute	Working	1	2/1/2017	.
Stephenson	In Aliquet Corporation	Working	4	11/14/2016	✓
Dalton	Diam Eu Dolor Corp.	Working	1	1/23/2017	.
Montoya	Dolor Industries	Working	2	11/4/2016	✓
Feager	International Shipping Co.	Reached	6	2/2/2016	✓
James	Delphi Chemicals	Reached	4	11/2/2016	✓
Harris	Diam Consulting	Reached	5	11/4/2016	✓

Figure 14.4 – Reporting on marketing SLA

Or perhaps you want to compare reps against each other. By dividing the number of *Tasks* with **IsConnect** checked by the total number of *Tasks*, you can find the connect rate percentage (figure 14.5).

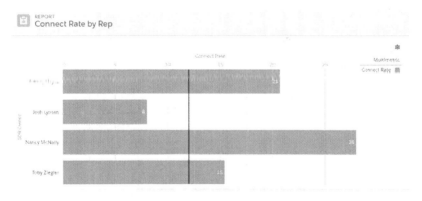

Figure 14.5 – Connect rate by rep report

This group's leader might want to talk to Josh Lyman about his low connect rate. Is he calling at the wrong times of day? Is he failing to gather enough direct dials? Or is he getting lower lead quality? You get the idea.

As a final example, you might track how many dials reps are making per prospect. You likely have a formal process—eight attempts before moving on for example—but are you reporting on it in Salesforce? Looking at the average number of dials across all prospects that were put through the full process gives you the clearest picture. Make sure to only include "Recycled" records where the **Recycled Reason** was set to "No Contact" in your report. This gives you the most accurate read of how many attempts reps are really making, since these prospects were never reached and, in theory, reps executed the full process in trying to reach them. Using these criteria, your report would return figure 14.6:

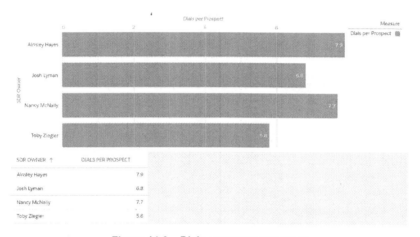

Figure 14.6 – Dials per prospect report

As you can see, Ainsley Hayes is at the SLA. While Toby Ziegler is well below. These data points can give SDR leaders valuable context to guide coaching conversations.

In a perfect world, your SDRs would go about their days making calls and working prospects. The *system* would handle the logging, classification, and analytics. With a few custom fields and the Process Builder outline above, you can get closer to that reality than ever before.

CHAPTER 15

⚡

MAKE WORKING IN SALESFORCE WORKABLE

RECENTLY, I RAN ACROSS A QUESTION on Salesforce Answers that asked:

> *Anyone using Salesforce to log daily outreach by a sales development team? I'd like to ultimately be able to report on how many "touches" our team has made each day. They outreach via phone and email, mostly.*
>
> *I don't want to slow them down, just want to log every attempt. We already use Tasks but need something faster! Just a click, to capture the date, really. Any ideas out there?*

Few reps have ever described prospecting in Salesforce as *fast*. They're more likely to call it "clunky." Or maybe "cumbersome." And even sometimes a total "cluster_____." With Lightning, you can finally(!) build a user experience that enables, and not encumbers, your reps. All without custom code and development. There are three pieces to this puzzle:

1. Customized Lightning Pages
2. Custom quick actions
3. Process and cadence (i.e., the number and rhythm of attempts your reps make)

Let's take them in order. Lighting Pages are custom layouts that you design for Salesforce1 mobile apps or pages in Lightning Experience. Pages are made up of drag and drop components that give admins far more control than

93

we've ever had in Salesforce Classic. So far in this book, you've seen partial screenshots of the *Lead* record page. Here is the entire custom Lightning Page in the editor view (figure 15.1):

Figure 15.1 – Lead Lightning Page

This page uses the header (1), subheader (2), and two columns (3.a & 3.b) template. I've workshopped a half dozen iterations of this page with various SDR teams. This orientation seems to be the most intuitive and user-friendly. The beauty of Pages is that you can choose a different template, reorder the components, or otherwise customize the page to suit your users' needs.

The second piece to the enablement puzzle is Actions. You'll use actions to save your reps from having to leave records and load another page to do something routine. This answers the need from the questioner mentioned above: *"I don't want to slow them down, just want to log every attempt. We already use Tasks but need something faster!"* Compare the "classic" experience of logging a call to the action in Lightning in figure 15.2.

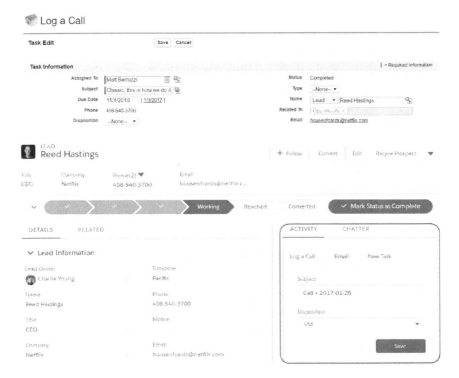

Figure 15.2 – Log a call in Classic (top) and Lightning custom action (bottom)

Beyond a more modern look and feel, there's real power in actions. Let's walk through logging a call in Classic. You click [Log a Call], a new page is loaded, you enter a subject, set the disposition, save, and return back the record where it all began. This takes roughly ten seconds. In Lightning, you needn't leave the record itself. You, as the admin, can prefill fields to save users clicks. As you can see, I've preset the **Subject** with a formula and defaulted the **Disposition** to "VM." In the example above, if you left Reed Hastings a voicemail, it's two clicks and you're done in under four seconds by my stopwatch.

Over the course of one thousand or more dials a month, these little things add up. A quick note about actions is to make sure you uncheck "Create Feed Item." If checked, each usage will post to Chatter and clog up the feed something horrific. The more you know. ✳

This is one area where the Lightning Experience really shines. If you're using Salesforce Classic, the common solution is to create a custom "Log a Call" button that shaves off a few clicks. This approach leverages URL hacking, which Salesforce has never officially supported. As such, I'll leave you in the hands of Dr. Google should you want to head down that road.

The third and final leg of this productivity tripod is an outreach cadence. By that I mean how many attempts a rep should be making to reach a prospect and how much time should pass between attempts. The traditional approach has been to document a process outside Salesforce and enforce/monitor it by requiring reps to manage open *Tasks*. As anyone who has ever been a sales development rep can attest, this approach is much more attractive in theory than in practice.

One of three things ends up happening. One, reps don't schedule follow-up tasks to avoid all the extra clicks and things get missed. Two, reps have a massive backlog of overdue tasks that they continually snooze. Or three, reps spend so much time meticulously managing open tasks that their call volume suffers.

Even at organizations that are strict about requiring open tasks, it is hard to measure how reps execute their cadence. "Out of the box, Salesforce doesn't guide reps on how to prospect. It is almost too freeform," shared Jay Schmidt, Inside Sales Manager SMB at Signiant. "Combine that with the fact that reps are coming into the role with less and less sales experience and it's too easy for reps to get into their own habits. The next thing you know, every SDR is doing something a little different."

Jay makes an important point. The beauty of Salesforce is the flexibility. The challenge with Salesforce—specifically for SDRs—is that same flexibility. Sales prospecting in Salesforce has traditionally been light on guidance and structure. The entire technology category I mentioned in the introduction is built, in part, to bridge this gap. While not a direct replacement, there is much that you can do to deliver on those goals natively within Salesforce. Customizing Lighting Pages and using Actions, as mentioned above, is one way. Building in structure through cadence automation is another.

Add Structure to Outreach

My advice is to leverage automation and avoid the *open tasks* trap entirely. Your reps should be logging calls, sending emails, and setting (important!) follow-up tasks as a matter of course. But automation should lead reps down the best path, providing structure and guidance. Specifically, your reps should use fields on records (*Leads* and *Contacts)—*not *Tasks—*to surface whom to call next and when to call them.

The biggest objection to the *no open tasks* approach is that things will get missed and valuable prospects will fall through the cracks. But, to me, using open tasks doesn't solve that problem. It only gives leaders a false sense of security. The presence of an open task doesn't guarantee follow-up any more than the presence of a dictionary guarantees good spelling. Reps and managers can stay better informed by referencing *automatically populated* fields like **Last Attempt Date**, **Last Connect Date**, and **# of Attempts**.

I worked with a client recently where the SDR leader wanted to address an issue with new leads not being worked fully. Their admin had built a report of "Leads with no future tasks" and sent it out to the team weekly. And you know what, things did change. Except, not in the way management had anticipated. It ended up that reps weren't making more attempts per prospect. They were simply creating and repeatedly pushing forward open tasks. Reps were able to keep off the "naughty" report without actually improving their prospecting behavior.

¯_(ツ)_/¯

A better approach is to monitor overdue *Leads*, not overdue *Tasks*.

In chapter 14, you saw how Process Builder can update a record when a call is logged. In that example, the updated fields included **# of Attempts**, **Last Activity Date**, and **Last Connect Date**. You can easily add a **Next Action Date** field to that list. We'll delve deeper into how to use **Next Action Date** and build out a cadence for your team in the next chapter. But before we do, I want to share the power this approach can provide in list views. In figure 15.3 below, I've used green checks, yellow alarms, and red flags to display **Cadence Status**—indicating whether a rep is on-target or behind in their outreach.

CADENCE STATUS	NAME	COMPANY ↑	NEXT ACTION DATE	# OF ATTEMPTS
☑	Phyllis Cotton	3CLogic	1/3/2017	
☑	Brenda Mcclure	Cadinal Inc.	1/3/2017	1
☑	Tom James	Delphi Chemicals	1/5/2017	4
◩	Sandra Eberhard	Highland Manufa...	11/28/2016	4
☑	Patricia Feager	International Ship...	1/4/2017	6
☑	Jeff Glimpse	Jackson Controls	1/6/2017	1
◩	Mike Braund	Metropolitan Heal...	11/22/2016	
◎	Acton Obrien	Nisi Institute	12/30/2016	1
◎	Bert	Trash	12/30/2016	2
☑	Bill Dadio Jr	Zenith Electronics	1/3/2017	3

Figure 15.3 – Visual cadence status indicator

For SDR managers, tracking status makes reporting and monitoring much more simple. Leaders can report on prospects that are "current," "overdue," and "*overdoom*!" These reports can be shared with Marketing for monitoring Service Level Agreement (SLA) compliance. Or you might use automation to send reps alerts when and if a prospect is accidentally left behind.

This isn't just for inbound leads, outbound prospecting requires the same—if not more—process stringency than inbound. Figure 15.4 below shows all *Leads* stacked to 100% by **Cadence Status**.

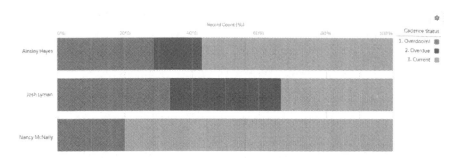

Figure 15.4 – Cadence status stacked to 100%

Instantly, you can see that Josh Lyman has fallen well behind. And Ainsley Hayes is trending in that direction. That's an example of quick and powerful insight you can deliver by reporting on outreach cadence. It's much more challenging to create similar reporting when relying on closed and open *Tasks*.

CHAPTER 16

⚡

FORMALIZE YOUR CADENCE

SO FAR WE'VE DISCUSSED using automation to update custom fields on *Leads* and *Contacts*. But we haven't covered *exactly how* reps should be managing their activities if they aren't using open tasks.

Liz Cain, VP of Go-to-Market Strategy at OpenView Venture Partners, shared her perspective with me. "I prefer to see reps working from list views. They can sort by the next time a rep plans to call with today's due leads at the top. They can see the date of their last activity and any 'SDR Next Step' notes. They can filter by lead source, campaign, or time zone. None of this requires leaving leads and fumbling with open activities."

To deliver Liz's vision, you need two things. First, you need to build your outreach cadence into Salesforce. Second, you need to create list views for reps to stay on top of their workloads.

The best SDR leaders work to find the optimal cadence for their teams. Your company might have several cadences—perhaps one for content marketing leads, another for named accounts, and another for demo requests. For our purposes let's use a simple example:

- ▶ Seven attempts
- ▶ Conducted over thirteen business days
- ▶ Making an attempt every other day
- ▶ 3 calls, 3 emails, and a LinkedIn message

Were this process to begin on a Monday, the cadence would look like figure 16.1:

Figure 16.1 – Seven attempt cadence

Once an "MQL" is assigned, automation would update the **Next Action Date** to today. Returning to your Process Builder on *Tasks*, you would add a line to the immediate update actions to populate the **Next Action Date** when a *Task* is logged. One important piece for the **Next Action Date** is that you want to avoid making tasks due on weekends. For example, if the first attempt was on Thursday, the second attempt should be due on Monday (not Saturday). This means you can't just add two days to the due date. If you did, reps would be facing three days' worth of due and overdue prospects every Monday morning. Not a great way to start each week.

Instead, you'll want to configure your logic to avoid weekends. Your seven attempts over thirteen business days would map to figure 16.2:

IF TODAY IS	NEXT ACTION ON
Monday	Wednesday
Tuesday	Thursday
Wednesday	Friday
Thursday	Monday
Friday	Tuesday

Figure 16.2 – Cadence and days of the week

Inside Process Builder (figure 16.3), you can use a formula to set the **Next Action Date** field.

```
TODAY() +
CASE( MOD( TODAY() - DATE(1900, 1, 7), 7), 4, 4, 5, 4, 2)
```

Essentially this formula begins by using January 7th, 1900—which was a Sunday—as a baseline. Then it subtracts that day from today. If the result is a "0" it means today is Sunday. If a "1," Monday. If a "2," Tuesday, etc. The formula then takes the current date and adds either four days, for Thursday and Friday, or two days for everything else. This formula doesn't take company holidays into account, but it's simple and works 99% of the time.

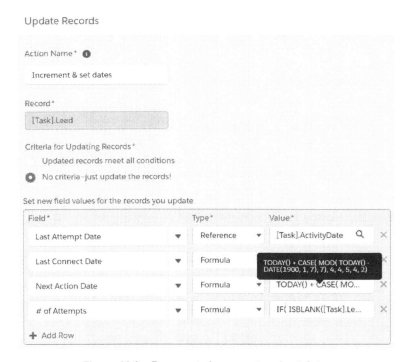

Figure 16.3 – Process to increment and set dates

Let's recap by way of an example. Say a rep comes in Monday morning and finds a brand new "MQL" assigned to them. They leave a voicemail and log a call via an action. Thanks to all your hard work, five things will now happen automatically:

1. A *Task* is created without leaving the record itself
2. The **Lead Status** is updated to "Working"
3. **# of Attempts** is set to "1" and **Last Attempt Date** is updated to today
4. **Next Action Date** is set for Wednesday
5. The **Cadence Status** formula field reflects a green checkmark to signify the rep is current

All of this runs behind the scenes. Automatically. Now that you've built your outreach cadence into Salesforce, it's time to guide reps on whom to contact and when to reach out.

Power Up Your List Views

Remember Jay Schmidt's comment from the previous chapter? Out of the box, Salesforce is almost too freeform. You'll use list views to add that prescriptive element to reps' workflows.

Again, imagine one of your inbound SDRs comes in Monday morning fired up and ready to go. She checks her calendar and doesn't have a scheduled call until after lunch. The next thing she wants to do is see how many new "MQLs" she's been assigned. She pops over to her "My New MQLs" list view (figure 16.4) and finds six new MQLs:

NAME ↑	TITLE	COMPANY	LAST CAMPAIGN	TIMEZONE
Althea Murphy	Technical P...	A Foundation	Formula & Analytics wi...	Mountain
Bertha Boxer	Director of ...	Farmers Coop. of Florida	Formula & Analytics wi...	Eastern
Calvin Frank	Interim IT ...	Scelerisque Dui Suspen...	DF16 session: Cheryl C...	Eastern
Celeste Waller	Managing ...	Tristique Incorporated	DF16 session: Cheryl C...	Eastern
Florence Sims	Vice Presid...	Pellentesque Associates	Formula & Analytics wi...	Pacific
Holly Horton	Systems En...	Sit Amet Inc.	WP: Meeting Room Bo...	Central
Isabelle Young	VP, Operati...	Vivamus Euismod Ltd	DF16 session: Cheryl C...	Eastern
Leah Blevins	Senior V.P	Nec Ante Ltd	Formulas for Fun & Pro...	Mountain
Mike Braund	VP, Techno...	Metropolitan Health Ser...	Formula & Analytics wi...	Eastern
Phyllis Cotton	CFO	3CLogic	Formulas for Fun & Pro...	Central
Raya Snow	Outside Sa...	Sit Amet Ornare Institute	Formula & Analytics wi...	Central
Vladimir Vale...	Director or...	Sed Pede Nec LLC	Top5 Channel Email Ca...	Pacific

Figure 16.4 – New MQL list view

Knowing that now is prime calling time for the East Coast, she decides to focus in the Eastern time zone. She finishes with those calls and reaches out to Central prospects next. Realizing it's still too early to call Pacific prospects, she decides to switch to her "My Active Prospects" list view (figure 16.5). Here she can see all her prospects and their **Next Action Dates**. She was out on PTO a few days last week and some of her **SDR Cadences** have gone red. She continues to work prospects from this list view. As she logs calls and send emails, the cadence fields update automatically.

CAD...	NAME	COMPANY	LEAD ST.	# OF AT...	LAST ATTEMPT...	NEXT ACTIO... ↑	TIMEZO...
📋	Sandra Eberhard	Highland Manufacturi...	Reached	4	11/15/2016	11/28/2016	Pacific
📋	Bertha Boxer	Farmers Coop. of Florida	MQL	3	11/4/2016	12/30/2016	Eastern
📋	Acton Obrien	Nisl Institute	Working	1	12/8/2016	12/30/2016	Eastern
✅	Phyllis Cotton	3CLogic	MQL		1/3/2017	1/3/2017	Central
✅	Brenda Mcclure	Cadinal Inc.	Working	1	11/3/2016	1/3/2017	Central
✅	Bill Dadio Jr	Zenith Electronics	Recycled	3	1/3/2017	1/3/2017	Eastern
✅	Patricia Feager	International Shipping ...	Reached	6	2/2/2016	1/4/2017	
✅	Tom James	Delphi Chemicals	Reached	4	11/2/2016	1/5/2017	Central
✅	Jeff Glimpse	Jackson Controls	Working	1	11/21/2016	1/6/2017	Eastern

Figure 16.5 – My active prospects list view

Or here's another approach. Say your SDRs want to bunch like actions together. You might build them a separate list view for each touch in the process (i.e., 1ˢᵗ Attempt, 2ⁿᵈ Attempt, 3ʳᵈ Attempt, etc.). This allows reps to gain efficiency by making a series of first calls one after the other. Then a group of second attempts, third attempts, etc. Your "2ⁿᵈ Attempt" list view might have the following criteria (see figure 16.6). In that list view, an SDR would see the subset of their prospects that are:

- On their second attempt (i.e., "1" for the **# of Attempts**)
- In either "Working" or "Reached" status
- Have a next action that is either due today or overdue

Figure 16.6 – 2ⁿᵈ attempt list view

In this scenario, your reps would hop between list views to determine whom to call next. Once a call was logged against a prospect in the "1ˢᵗ Attempt" list view, it would disappear from that view. Then two days later—again assuming the cadence is to make an attempt every other day—the prospect would appear in the "2ⁿᵈ Attempt" view. Prospects automatically move between the list views as calls and emails are logged. So on and so forth until the prospect is either qualified or recycled back to marketing.

Before we leave this topic, there's one final list view I want to mention. All credit goes to Amyra Rand, who earlier shared her take on the science of sales development. One of the challenges of a dedicated inbound SDR team is keeping each rep fully utilized. There are natural peaks and valleys in lead volume. I was discussing this issue with Amyra and she mentioned the concept of "if you've got time to lean, you've got time to clean." Her suggestion was to build a list of prospects that would be a level three focus—meaning once new MQLs (level 1) and active prospects (level 2) have been worked.

What makes up this tier of prospect will vary company to company. Here are a few examples to get you started:

- ▶ Contact Us prospects that were never reached
- ▶ Trials that ended thirty days ago
- ▶ Recent webinar attendees (who are just below the MQL threshold)

If an SDR completely catches up on their cadences, you don't want them to have to dig around for other prospects to contact. A rep could spend twenty minutes running reports to build a calling list. It's better to have a "time to lean" list view at the ready.

Use Data to Hone Your Cadence

Now that we've covered how to automate your outreach cadence and how to surface the right prospect at the right time, an obvious question remains. *How exactly do you know how many attempts your reps should be making?*

Studies have found that it takes between six and ten attempts (including at least four phone calls) to properly prospect a given contact. Consider the following from InsideSales.com:

> *The absolute bare minimum number of attempts to contact at least 50 percent of your leads is 6. The average rep's performance? Between 1.7 and 2.1 attempts before they give up.*
>
> *—Insidesales.com: How Many Contact Attempts*

Perhaps six to ten attempts is the right number for your sales development team. Or perhaps it's eleven. Or maybe it's only six for inbound and a full fourteen for outbound prospecting. The point is you don't know without looking at the data.

Jim McDonough, who earlier shared his *Account*-centric approach for prospecting strategic accounts, commented, "For a high-priority lead, like a trial, there should be a high volume of attempts. With someone who downloads an ebook and are much earlier on in their buyer's journey, fewer attempts might be more appropriate. We don't want the SDR coming at them like a ton of bricks. It's about using logic and data to find the optimal approach." Since you're tracking **Lead Status**, **Contact Status**, and **# of Attempts**, you have all the data you need to run reports and find the answer.

You can create a report of all records that are in either "Qualified" or "Recycled" status. (You don't want to skew the data with prospects that reps are still working.) Next, you'll group the report by **# of Attempts** and create a custom summary formula to return the "Qualification Rate" (i.e., the number of qualified records divided by the total number of records). Figure 16.7 below shows the results for one particular campaign source.

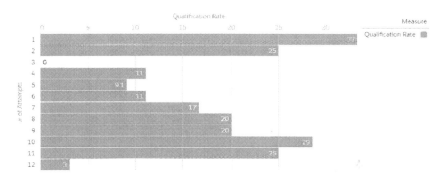

Figure 16.7 – Qualification rate by attempts

The chart suggests that ten is the optimal number of attempts. Efforts beyond that appear to have diminishing returns. You will likely see a peak at *one or two attempts*. This is to be expected. Sometimes prospects are able to be passed or reply "thanks but no thanks" early on in the process. It's rare, but it happens. Even though the qualification rate for these is high, the raw number of these instances are likely to be very low.

Once again, this is the power of "medium-sized" data. You're taking the byproduct of rep prospecting, namely loads and loads of *Task* records, and turning it into actionable intelligence.

By implementing the ideas we've covered in the last few chapters, you're laying the groundwork to change the trajectory of your SDR team. You're creating massive value for your reps to act more efficiently, for sales leadership to improve productivity, and for your whole organization to leverage insight and intelligence. Not bad for some custom fields, a few Process Builders, and a report or two.

PART 4

QUALIFY

Good fences make good neighbors.

—OLD PROVERB

CHAPTER 17

⚡

ROUTE MEETINGS ROUND-ROBIN

IN PARTS 1-3, we worked through the identification, planning, and contact portions of the SDR workflow. Next, we'll turn our attention to qualification. There are four key components to the qualification and handoff process:

1. Assigning meetings to the correct account executives (AEs)
2. Ensuring that qualification criteria are met
3. Passing the meeting itself
4. Closing the loop, post-handoff

There is a bit of a debate in the sales development space about the best way to align inbound SDRs with their AE counterparts. Do you partner SDR A with AE 1 and AE 2? Or do SDR A and SDR B rotate their meetings evenly between AEs 1-4? From an implementation perspective, directly linking SDRs to AEs is easiest. If AEs are assigned geographic territories, SDRs can draw from memory or reference printed maps when scheduling meetings.

But from a business perspective, it isn't so clear.

The case for distributing SDR meetings round-robin mirrors the logic for rotating inbound leads: *equity.* One VP of sales put it to me this way. "Our focus is on evening the playing field for closing rep performance. We want to make sure that all account executives receive equal SDR support. At the same time, we want to avoid a situation where a bad SDR or bad AE can drag down and demotivate the other member of that team."

This approach works best with inbound sales development groups. For outbound SDRs, and particularly in an account-based selling strategy, all oars need to be rowing in the same direction. In that instance, directly pairing one or more SDRs with one or more AEs is more appropriate.

From my conversations with sales development leaders and Salesforce admins, I'd estimate that one-third to one-half of companies have adopted round-robin distribution for meetings set by inbound SDRs. For those that have gone round-robin, one clear thing stands out in particular. *Companies are using some pretty kludgy methods to manage the assignment piece.*

Some companies use whiteboards where SDRs will stand up and peek over to see who's "up next." Let's not forget that written language—at roughly 3,000 years old—was the first sales acceleration technology. A handful of companies are using Google Sheets to make that whiteboard process electronic. One of my favorites was an "Even Steven" report, where reps could check to see who was behind in meetings and assign them the next one.

These are some pretty impressive hacks. You should admire their creativity, but not seek to replicate them.

What you should do is make this round-robin process seamless inside Salesforce. One approach is something I call *the deli ticket*. You know those little paper tickets that are dispensed at the deli? You "please take a number" and wait till you're up on the "now serving" board. It's just like that. You can build automation into Salesforce that runs in fundamentally the same way. It makes use of a few key pieces:

- ▶ A custom *Deli Ticket* object
- ▶ Process Builder to kick off the automation
- ▶ A Flow to find the "Now Serving" AE, collect their ticket, and assign who's next

Build Your Deli Tickets

To keep things simple, imagine you have seven account executives on your sales team. They are generalists and aren't specialized by vertical, company size, or any other factors. Your goal is to make sure that for every seven SDR-sourced meetings, each AE receives one meeting. Your *Deli Ticket* custom object might look like figure 17.1 below:

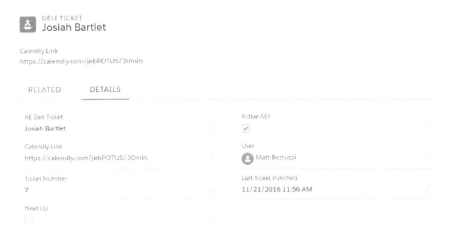

Figure 17.1 – Deli ticket custom object

Notice a few key fields. The **Active AE** checkbox can be used to take account executives out of rotation—for vacation, family leave, sabbatical, and so on. Thanks to Kevin Dorsey at SnackNation for the suggestion of adding the **Calendly Link** directly on the record. This gives your SDRs one-click access to the free/booked times on a given AE's calendar. The **User** field is, unsurprisingly, a look-up for the *User* object. That will come in handy later on for assigning records to the appropriate AE.

Also, notice the **Next Up** checkbox which designates which *Deli Ticket* will receive the next meeting. This gives your SDR Manager the ability to override the automation and designate who is up next. Say, for example, a poorly qualified meeting gets passed—one that never should have made it through. You wouldn't want to penalize that AE and have them out of the rotation until the next round of meetings. With this checkbox, you as the admin have (or can share) the flexibility to handle these types of circumstances.

Figure 17.2 gives you a view of all seven AEs. You can see that "Danny Concannon" is out of the rotation and that "Matt Santos" is next up to receive a meeting.

ACTIV...	AE DELI TICKET	TICKE... ↑	NEXT...	LAST TICKET PUNCHED
✓	Charlie Young	1	☐	11/20/2016 9:53 AM
✓	CJ Craig	2	☐	11/29/2016 9:24 AM
✓	Dolores Landing...	3	☐	11/25/2016 5:56 PM
✓	Donnatella Moss	4	☐	11/25/2016 8:12 AM
✓	Matt Santos	5	✓	11/22/2016 8:30 AM
☐	Danny Concannon	6	☐	11/23/2016 1:50 PM
✓	Josiah Bartlet	7	☐	11/21/2016 11:56 AM

Figure 17.2 – Deli Ticket list view

Okay, you've built a custom object to handle the ticketing. Great. Now, you need to determine how and when meetings are "served" to the next *Deli Ticket* holder.

I prefer to not assign the AE before the meeting is booked. If you were to pre-assign on either MQL or first live connect, you would again encounter the issue of inequitable round-robin. Since not every live connect results in a meeting, more AEs would be assigned than meetings would be booked. Again, just by random chance, that would mean that some AEs get more meetings than others. Not good! For that reason, you shouldn't pre-assigned AEs to every prospect "MQL'd" by marketing.

You might consider creating an **Assign an AE** checkbox field on *Leads* and *Contacts*. When the prospect has agreed to a meeting, the SDR would check the box and save. Then Process Builder would call a Flow to handle all the heavy lifting. As your SDRs are asking the prospect to bring up their own calendar, they check the box, save, and the "next up" AE is assigned. Then, the rep can hover over **Assigned AE** to link to the relevant account executive's calendar (figure 17.3).

Company		Email
Jackson Controls		jeffo@jackson.com
LinkedIn URL	Josiah Bartlet	Story
https://www.lin		
Assigned AE	Calendly Link	AE
Josiah Bartlet	https://calendly.com/jebP...	

Figure 17.3 – Calendly link on hover

This *checkbox* ⟶ *Process Builder* ⟶ *Flow* automation may sound a bit clunky. But all the work is done "off-stage." For the SDRs where I've deployed this, it quickly becomes second nature. To bring this all together, your Flow needs to do a few things:

1. Find the "next up" *Deli Ticket*

2. Update the **Assigned AE** field on the originating *Lead* or *Contact*

3. Uncheck the **Next Up** field and stamp the **Last Ticket Punched** date/time on that *Deli Ticket*

4. Find the *Deli Ticket* that should receive the next meeting and check its **Next Up** box

Your flow for handling *Deli Tickets* might look like figure 17.4 below. We're using a few decision elements to handle any exceptions—say when the "next up" rep isn't active or when we punch ticket #7 and need to restart back at #1. The linked YouTube video will give you a walkthrough and explanation (http://sdrbook.io/deliticket - all lowercase).

Let's just pause for a moment to reflect on how impressive the Visual Workflow engine is. Two years ago, automation like this was 100% outside the scope of any *button-click* Salesforce admin. Today, we can handle this scenario natively without any development resources. We live in very interesting times indeed.

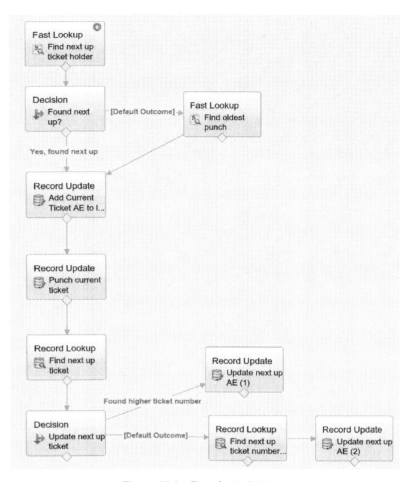

Figure 17.4 – Flow for deli tickets

CHAPTER 18

⚡

MAKE QUALIFICATION BINARY

OVER AND AGAIN in conversations with sales, marketing, and SDR leaders, I heard a common refrain: *qualification criteria need to be binary.* There should be no messy middle as to whether an SDR-set meeting was ready to be passed or not.

"You want to avoid a situation where you're playing hot potato," shared Kristin Agnelli Senior Director of Lead Development at PGi. "If your SDR comes to you and says, 'I set up this opportunity and it met all the criteria, but the sales rep told me it's not good enough.' That's a big problem. You need to make the qualification criteria black and white. Put those fields inside your CRM. Make the process easy to track and measure. That's the only way to consistently hold people accountable."

Ambiguous criteria can lead to subjective interpretation and a messy handoff. Say you have variation between what individual AEs consider passable. Now, your SDRs are trying to aim at a moving target. Or say you have variation in the level of qualification between SDRs. Now, you're frustrating your account executives when and if they get handed "weak" opportunities. Both can cause major tension between the groups. And since much of SDR compensation is driven by these metrics, it is serious business.

This isn't to say that you must have one, single qualification for every type of meeting. You might require looser criteria for larger opportunities, for example. Or perhaps you might require a higher degree of qualification on inbound versus outbound meetings. The point is that SDRs should be crystal clear on when a prospect does—and doesn't—meet the criteria. "We use the

CHAMP framework (CHallenges, Authority, Money, and Priority) for qualification," shared Phill Keene Manager of Demand Generation at Octiv. "When a prospect has met three of those four criteria, it is ready to be passed. We've added a visual indicator in Salesforce to make it crystal clear."

Let's take Phill's approach and apply it to our conference room display and scheduling software example. To refresh your memory, we've built a "Qualification Information" section (figure 18.1):

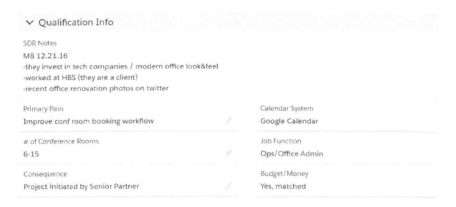

Figure 18.1 – Qualification information section

Imagine that you have two qualification rules. For prospects with fewer than 15 conference rooms, all six fields are required *plus* the budget must match our price point. For 16+ conference rooms, the "consequence of inaction" can be blank and a matched budget isn't required. We have two options. We can use a validation rule to prevent passing a prospect that fails to meet the criteria. Or we can use a visual cue to indicate when the prospect is or isn't pass-able.

Often, validation rules feel about as subtle as a slap to the face. Let's say you're heading to a new restaurant that doesn't allow baseball caps to be worn. Which would you prefer? A burly bouncer putting his hand on your shoulder and scolding "no hats!" (like a validation rule) or a sign in the foyer indicating caps should be removed?

As I'm sure you've guessed, I prefer the second option.

An image formula field is an easy way to provide that visual cue. The formula won't be pretty, but you can code the logic above into a **Ready to Pass** field. It might look like figure 18.2 below. If the criteria are met, the formula returns a green handshake. And if not, a yellow warning icon.

```
IF(
  ISBLANK(TEXT(of_Conference_Rooms__c)), NULL,
  IF(
  ((ISPICKVAL(of_Conference_Rooms__c, "< 5") ||
  ISPICKVAL(of_Conference_Rooms__c, "6-15")) &&
  NOT(ISBLANK(Primary_Pain__c) || ISBLANK(TEXT(Calendar_System__c))
||
  ISBLANK(TEXT(Job_Function__c)) || ISBLANK(Consequence__c))
  && ISPICKVAL(Budget_Money__c, "Yes, matched"))
  ||
  ((ISPICKVAL(of_Conference_Rooms__c, "16-30") ||
  ISPICKVAL(of_Conference_Rooms__c, "31+")) &&
  NOT(ISBLANK(Primary_Pain__c) || ISBLANK(TEXT(Calendar_System__c))
||
  ISBLANK(TEXT(Job_Function__c)))),
  IMAGE("/logos/Custom/Handshake_Green/logo.png", "Green", 20, 20),
  IMAGE("/logos/Custom/Triangle_Yellow/logo.png", "Yellow", 20, 20)
))
```

∨ Qualification Info

SDR Notes
MB 12.21.16
-they invest in tech companies / modern office look&feel
-worked at HBS (they are a client)
-recent office renovation photos on twitter

Primary Pain
Improve conf room booking workflow

Calendar System
Google Calendar

# of Conference Rooms
6-15

Job Function
Ops/Office Admin

Consequence
Project initiated by Senior Partner

Budget/Money
Yes, matched

Ready to Pass?

Meeting Date

Figure 18.2 – Ready to pass indicator

You might still need to create a validation rule to prevent passing these meetings. But at least you've given your reps a chance to avoid the harsh scolding. *No hats!*

There's another benefit to putting qualification fields inside Salesforce that I'd like to highlight: *guidance and course correction*. By mapping these fields onto *Opportunities*, you can now compare your qualification criteria to actual wins and losses. You can begin to model which types of meetings have a high-probability of closing versus which types are low-probability.

In the early stages of a group, initial qualification criteria are partly a best guess. You're asking the Sales team what types of meetings they would like to be delivered. All this assumes what "they want" is the same as what "they need." Often, that assumption is correct. But nearly as often, you'll have to adjust your criteria based on data. Trust, but verify is the sales operations code. Again, Kristin Agnelli shares her insight. "You might find that your meetings are being accepted, but when you dig deeper, there's limited revenue tied to them. Having these fields inside CRM helps you answer, *What might we be missing?* Are we losing at the lower-end? Is there a technical or political challenge we need to be screening for? Ultimately, you're looking for the qualification methodology that puts the highest volume of winnable deals into the pipeline."

Returning to our example, you want to be able to report on win rate across a number of factors: *number of conference rooms, calendar system, primary pain point, and so on*. Figure 18.3 presents the results.

REPORT
Win Rate Matrix: by #rooms & calendar

Win Rate
33%

CALENDAR SYSTEM	EXCHANGE 2013	GOOGLE CALENDAR	ICLOUD	OFFICE 365	NONE	Total
# OF CONFERENCE ROOMS	WIN RATE	WIN RATE	WIN RATE	WIN RATE	WIN RATE	WIN RATE
< 5	0%	50%	0%	·	0%	25%
6-15	0%	0%	0%	·	20%	12%
16-30	100%	56%	0%	·	0%	47%
31+	33%	67%	0%	100%	0%	36%
Total	38%	53%	0%	100%	9%	33%

Figure 18.3 – Win rate matrix report

In this example, you can see that the "Win Rate" is much higher for prospects with a greater **# of Conference Rooms**—nearly triple that of those with fewer than 16 rooms.

You can also see that using "Exchange 2013" or "Google Calendar" for prospecting is a strong point, but there are lower win rates on accounts with no formal calendaring system and those using "iCloud." This suggests that, perhaps, the qualification criteria should be changed to maximize both SDR and AE productivity. You might make the criteria stricter for *small, non-Exchange/non-Google* accounts. And loosen it a bit for the reverse.

This back-end reporting is only made possible by having SDRs populate this data on the front end.

CHAPTER 19

⚡

BUILD FOR A SMOOTH HANDOFF

NO ONE EXPECTS that every single SDR-sourced meeting will make it into AE pipeline. At least I *hope* no one does. Our research at The Bridge Group shows a 55-80% acceptance rate depending on qualification criteria (i.e. "introductory meeting" versus "fully qualified opportunity"). The key to accurate measurement lies in standardizing the hand-off process.

There are many ways to "hand-off" meetings inside Salesforce. In my experience the most common include:

▶ Modifying *Tasks* or *Events* to track the meetings

▶ Building a custom "meeting" object

▶ Using the native *Opportunities* object

I feel very strongly that the third approach, *Opportunities*, is the best choice as it allows for easier SDR hand-off, better AE workflow, and more accurate reporting.

Using non-*Opportunity* objects requires SDRs and AEs to create, assign, and edit special "tracking" records. It is too easy for these little things to fall through the cracks. Since every account executive uses *Opportunities* heavily, this approach meets them where they're already working.

If you let AEs create *Opportunities* after a successful SDR-sourced meeting, there's still no way to guarantee data integrity. Should the AE create an *Opportunity* from the *Account*, the SDR information and campaign history is lost. Should they create from another *Contact* (i.e., meeting was with the IT

Director and the AE created the *Opportunity* off the CIO), again the SDR information and campaign history is lost. The cleanest, simplest, and most accurate approach involves SDRs creating "Stage 0: Pre-Opportunities."

Often, sales leadership and account executives will object that they don't want SDR-sourced opportunities "clogging up the pipeline" and "muddying the forecast." If you encounter this objection, here are two responses you can share. First, more than half of SDR-sourced meetings will be accepted into Stage 1 pipeline. It creates extra work and risks breaking the reporting chain to use a non-*Opportunity* object. Why risk that for a minority of instances? Second, you'll be creating "Stage 0: Pre-Opportunities" that sit apart from "real" sales opportunities. A clear, bright line will separate SDR-passed meetings and AE-accepted opportunities. These pre-opportunities will be excluded from forecast, pipeline, and win-loss reporting.

Hopefully, that background should calm any jangly nerves from the sales team.

We'll discuss automating the handoff in the next chapter, but for now, let's focus on building the underlying infrastructure. In reality, your "Pre Opportunities" are still *Opportunity* records—but with a separate record type, a different sales process, and an entirely different look and feel. The beauty of the "Stage 0: Pre-Opportunity" approach is how simple it makes things for the account executives. After a successful meeting, AEs are a few clicks away from promoting a "Pre-Opportunity" to a real one. Figure 19.1 compares the "Pre-Opportunity" with the full, familiar *Opportunity*.

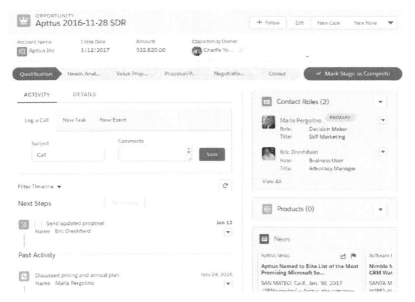

Figure 19.1 – Stage 0: Pre-Opportunity (top) and full Opportunity (bottom)

Notice how differently those two records appear. Different stages, different related lists, and different components on the page. There's no amount, no close date, no products, etc. This is a feature, not a bug. The fact that these "Stage 0: Pre-Opportunities" don't look like normal *Opportunities* is what makes the approach work. By creating any entirely different look and feel account executives and sales leaders tend to be a lot less resistant to the idea of SDRs creating *Opportunities*. I have no idea why, but I'll take a win by hook or by crook.

Your "Pre-Opportunities" will require a bit of infrastructure. As a first step, you'll want to create two new *Opportunity* **Stages**.

STAGE	DESCRIPTION	PROB. %	FORECAST CATEGORY
SDR-Sourced	A meeting passed by an SDR to an AE	0%	Omitted
Closed No Oppty	An SDR-sourced meeting that didn't convert to pipeline	0%	Omitted

Figure 19.2 – New opportunity stages

"SDR-Sourced" will be the default value for new meetings from the SDR team. It will reflect a 0% probability and be in the "Omitted" **Forecast Category**—meaning that these "Pre-Opportunities" won't show up in pipeline and forecast reviews. "Closed No Oppty" will be used when an account executive rejects an SDR-sourced meeting. You can use standard "Closed/Lost" for this, but I prefer a separate value. It is easy enough to create "Closed No Oppty," exclude it from sales win/loss analysis, and include it in SDR-results reporting.

Next, you can create a new Sales Process called "Pre-Opportunity" (see figure 19.3 below). As a reminder, Salesforce Sales Processes "*contain the Stages an Opportunity follows through its sales cycle.*" When a meeting is booked and a "Pre-Opportunity" is created, the sales process will only have three available stages. Meetings will come in at Stage 0 "SDR-Sourced." The AEs can either *accept* them, and change to Stage 1 "Qualification," or *reject* them, and change to "Closed No Oppty."

Figure 19.3 – Pre-Opportunity sales process

You'll also want to create an "SDR Pre-Opportunity" record type and associate it with the "Pre-Opportunity" Sales Process above. Finally, you can turn to building a page layout and a lightning page specifically for these records. Picking up our conference room display and scheduling software example, your record page might look like figure 19.4:

Figure 19.4 – SDR Pre-Opportunity Lightning page

Notice this page is presenting just the three **Stages** that are available to this record type (1). All the qualification details are presented for the AE to review (2). There is one click access to both the *Account* and the *Contact* via the contact role (3). When an account executive changes the **Stage** from "SDR-Sourced" to "Qualification," you can use Process Builder to update the record type. That change in record type will result in an entirely different look and feel for the *Opportunity* itself. Not to geek out too hard here, but that's friggin' awesome.

In Salesforce Classic, you can control which fields and related lists appear via the page layout. All other customizations are the domain of developers and Visualforce. But in Lightning, you can control which components of the page are present and when/where they appear. Amazing.

Before we get into the details of how to create "Stage 0: Pre-Opportunities," I want to spend a few moments on Path and *Opportunities*.

Leverage Path

As we covered in chapter 13, Path combines a *distance-to-goal* visual element with the ability to surface key fields and offer stage-specific guidance. For these "Stage 0: Pre-Opportunities," you might configure a path as follows:

STATUS	FIELDS
SDR-Sourced	*None*
Qualification	Amount, Close Date
Closed No Oppty	Rejection Reason, Rejection Notes

Figure 19.5 – Path on opportunities

For an AE to accept a "Pre-Opportunity", they would add an **Amount**, adjust the **Close Date**, and change the **Stage to** "Qualification" (see figure 19.6 below). You should add a validation rule to enforce these required fields.

Figure 19.6 – Accepting a pre-opportunity

To reject a "Stage 0: Pre-Opportunity," they would add a **Rejection Reason** and **Rejection Notes** (figure 19.7). I recommend you require both a reason and notes for rejection. These two fields present the SDRs with crucial feedback. This gives the manager a "coaching moment" to begin a dialogue about what the rep might do differently the next time.

Additionally, as you'll see in the following chapter, you can email the rep and the SDR leader on rejection. Again, you should add a validation rule to enforce required fields.

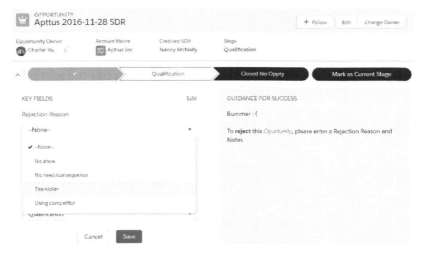

Figure 19.7 – Rejecting a pre-opportunity

If you're using Salesforce Classic, relying on Path isn't an option. In that case, I recommend using a flow initiated by an [Accept / Reject] button. The flow will walk AEs through the steps to accept or reject. Your flow might look like figure 19.8 below and guide reps to provide required information. The linked YouTube video will give you a walkthrough and explanation (http://sdrbook.io/acceptreject - all lowercase).

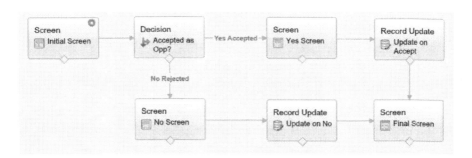

Figure 19.8 – Accept or reject flow

Automate Pre-Opportunity Creation from Contacts

Assuming your SDRs are working *Accounts & Contacts*, you'll want to ensure that *Opportunities* can only be created from *Contacts*. Not from the Account. Not from the [New] button on the *Opportunity* tab. And not from <shudder> Quick Create. This is somewhere between a "best practice" and Salesforce admin commandment. *Opportunities* that aren't created from *Contacts*—or *Leads*—muck up the reporting chain royally.

Mallory Lee is a consultant to high-growth marketing organizations. She shared, "I want all opportunities created from a contact. This is something I'm more strict on than most. This does a few important things. It creates a contact role, brings over campaign history, and allows for campaign influence measurement. We all know that the marketing funnel is long and multi-touch. The best way to evaluate campaigns is to track everything that happens in the lifetime of a lead. You can't do that without a connection between the opportunity and contact."

I could not agree with Mallory more. Getting reps to consistently add *Contact Roles* to their deals is about as easy as potty-training a Cape Buffalo. Block as many other ways as possible, and your users will default to creating *Opportunities* from their *Contacts* as the path of least resistance.

As it stands today, I'm not in love with the experience of creating a new *Opportunity* from a *Contact* in Lightning. This is one area where I think Salesforce has taken a step backwards. There has been some discussion with Salesforce Product Management on the *Success Community* about improving this workflow in future releases. Fingers crossed! Today, the process to create an *Opportunity* from a *Contact* includes:

▶ Navigating to the related list

▶ Clicking for a [New] *Opportunity*

▶ Indicating you indeed intended to create a "New Opportunity"

▶ Creating the *Opportunity* itself; including selecting the correct *Account* (why!?!) and filling the relevant fields

▶ Selecting the role of the *Opportunity Contact Role*

Sadly, we can't use an Opportunity Action to shortcut this process. My recommendation is to go 100% automated with an autolaunched flow. You might add a **Create SDR Pre-Oppty** checkbox on the *Contact* object that, once checked, uses Process Builder to call a flow. Or you might fully automate the new "Pre-Opportunity" when the **Contact Status** reaches "Qualified."

Or, if you prefer, you can choose to leave it to reps to create *Opportunities* manually. Perhaps your reps are in the top 1% for detail-oriented Salesforce users. If so, I envy you! For the rest of us, there are too many steps and too many points of failure for data integrity. Better to leverage automation.

The flow is straightforward (see figure 19.9). The **Contact ID** is passed in from Process Builder. The flow itself (1) creates a new *Opportunity* bringing over all relevant SDR and qualification information, (2) creates an *Opportunity Contact Role* linking the *Contact* and the *Opportunity*, and (3) updates the **Opportunity Owner** to the **Assigned AE**. The linked YouTube video will give you a walkthrough and explanation (http://sdrbook.io/contacttooppty - all lowercase).

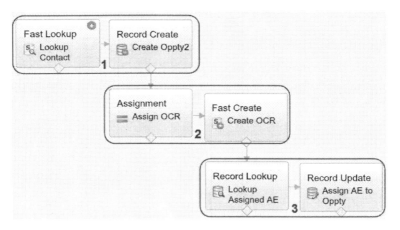

Figure 19.9 – Flow to create pre-opportunity from a contact

Now your SDRs are just a click and save away from booking the meeting with the *Contact* and creating a fully-loaded "Pre-Opportunity" (figure 19.10).

CONTACT
Maria Pergolino

Name
Maria Pergolino

Account Phone
1-650-445-7700

Title
SVP Marketing

Phone
415-856-5110

Account Name
 Apttus Inc

Mobile

Assigned AE
Charlie Young

Email
notmaria@apttus.com

∨ Qualification Info

SDR Notes
11/25 NM- great call with Maria. Big google shop. Open concept office and hard to collaborate at desks. Wants demo from AE.

Primary Pain
Instantly find & book open conf ✏️
rooms

Calendar System
Google Calendar

# of Conference Rooms
16-30

Budget/Money
Yes, matched

Ready to Pass?
🗨️

Meeting Date
11/30/2016

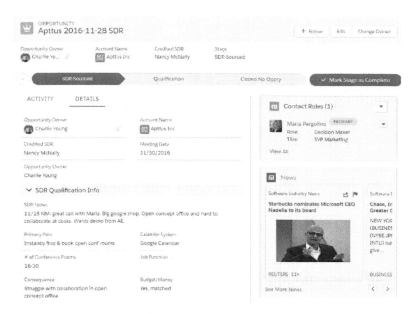

Figure 19.10 – The *Contact* (top) and Pre-Opportunity (bottom)

Automate Pre-Opportunity Creation from Leads

Creating *Opportunities* on lead conversion is a much smoother process out of the box. The SDR would select a converted **Status**, match or create a new *Account*, and name their new *Opportunity*. Easy peasy.

Here, you can use "lead custom field mapping" (to move the qualification information) and Process Builder (to pre-fill the remaining relevant *Opportunity* fields). Note, to save the SDRs from having to click through to the *Opportunity* and reassign the record to the appropriate AE, I use a few hidden fields. **AE Id** on *Leads* can store the 18-digit user ID for the **Assigned AE**. **AE Id from Leads** on *Opportunities* can receive that user ID via lead custom field mapping (figure 19.11 below).

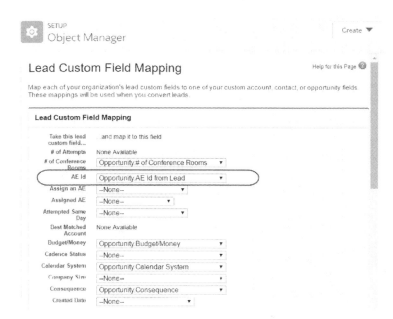

Figure 19.11 – Lead custom field mapping

Once an SDR has converted a *Lead* and created the *Opportunity*, Process Builder will handle the rest (see figure 19.12 below). Specifically, it will rename the *Opportunity*, add the **Credited SDR**, and update the **Opportunity Owner** to the correct AE.

I've worked with several companies that moved from passing meetings as *Events* to utilizing "Stage 0: SDR Pre-Opportunities." The feedback has been overwhelming positive. For both the SDRs and AEs, "it just works." And for marketing and sales operations, it leads to easier and more accurate analysis. In the next chapter, we'll discuss notifying, monitoring, and reporting on these SDR-sourced meetings.

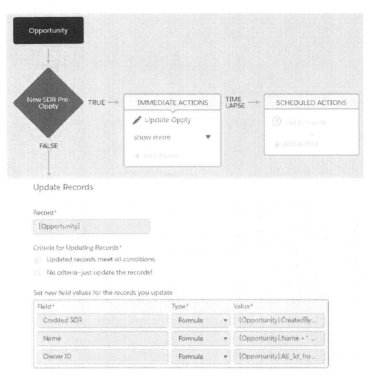

Update Records

Record*

[Opportunity]

Criteria for Updating Records*

- Updated records meet all conditions
- No criteria—just update the records!

Set new field values for the records you update

Field*	Type*	Value*
Credited SDR	Formula ▾	[Opportunity].CreatedBy...
Name	Formula ▾	[Opportunity].Name + "...
Owner ID	Formula ▾	[Opportunity].AE_Id_fro...

Figure 19.12 – Process to update to pre-opportunity

135

CHAPTER 20

⚡

ADD CHECKS AND BALANCES

NOW THAT YOU HAVE BUILT THE INFRASTRUCTURE for "Stage 0: Pre-Opportunities," it's time to move on to other considerations. The first of which is notification. There are several key moments in the life of an SDR-sourced *Opportunity*: creation, acceptance or rejection, and (hopefully) closing as a win. Each require a slightly different notification medium and serve a slightly different audience. You can use the figure 20.1 below as a starting point:

MOMENT	MEDIUM	AUDIENCE
Pre-Oppty Created	Email	Assigned Account Executive
Accepted	Chatter	*"SDR Ring the Gong!"* Chatter group
Rejected	Email	SDR and their manager
Closed Won	Chatter + Email	SDRs and SDR leadership, AE, SVP of Sales, etc."

Figure 20.1 – Alter media and audiences

My general philosophy is to post good news (atta-boys and atta-girls) publicly. And to share bad news (meeting rejection) privately over email. You can use Process Builder to post to Chatter and to send emails for each instance. You should strongly consider creating a public Chatter group for the

136

SDRs, SDR managers, and sales leadership. Chatter is a great way to virtually ring the gong and publicly celebrate wins (see figure 20.2).

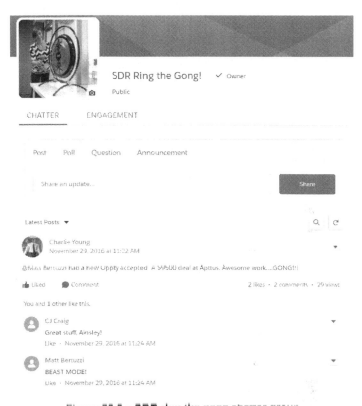

Figure 20.2 – SDR ring the gong chatter group

In the example above, a Chatter post was automatically created when the AE accepted the "Pre-Opportunity." When an SDR-sourced opportunity is won, you might use Process Builder to post to this Chatter group *and* send a congratulatory email up the food chain. Depending on how many SDRs you have—and the volume of wins per week—you might include the SDR manager, the VP of sales, CMO, and even the CEO on that email.

Now that we've covered notification, let's turn our attention to monitoring.

Even though the "Stage 0: Pre-Opportunity" approach provides an easier and better user experience, you should still build in at least one guardrail. As every Salesforce admin knows, a *user* is defined as someone with both

Salesforce access and an inexplicable ability to break even the most carefully constructed process. As the old CRM saying might go, *you can lead a rep to opportunity, but you can't make them click.*

In chapter 13, we discussed time-to-contact and number of attempts as components of the marketing-SDR Service Level Agreement (SLA). Another SLA deals with the account executives' responsibilities to their SDR counterparts. Specifically, your AEs should commit to accepting or rejecting a "Pre-Opportunity" within a day of the meeting. Since you're tracking the **Meeting Date**, you can use a time-based workflow rule. Like all time-dependent workflows, this rule will fire on save and remain queued until processed or the rule criteria are evaluated as false. As long as your AEs change the **Stage** to either "Qualification" or "Close No Oppty," the reminder emails won't fire.

As an added line of defense, you might consider using an escalating reminder approach. The first email reminds the AE, a second email copies in the SDR, and a third email copies in the SDR's and AE's managers (see figure 20.3).

Figure 20.3 – Email reminder workflow rule

Perhaps all this seems a bit heavy handed to you. I totally get it. But these little details are the difference between a *not worth the paper it's written on* SLA and one that's been put into practice.

Now that your SDRs and AEs are comfortable with "Pre-Opportunities," it's time to build in tracking capabilities. You can create two custom fields on the *Opportunity* object. First, you can create an **AE Accepted Date** field to capture, not surprisingly, the date an AE accepted the opportunity into stage 1 pipeline. Second, you can create an **IsAccepted** checkbox formula field as follows:

```
NOT( ISBLANK( AE_Accept_Date__c ))
```

This formula will return FALSE (unchecked) if the **AE Accepted Date** is blank. And TRUE (checked) when it is populated. In your reporting, you can report on "Acceptance Rate" since checkbox fields can be used in formulas. Be sure to exclude records where the **Stage** is still "SDR-Sourced" as these will skew the reporting. You should also add a custom summary formula to the report that divides your **IsAccepted** field by the total number of records:

```
(Opportunity.Accepted_by_AE__c:SUM / RowCount)
```

Your results might resemble figure 20.4.

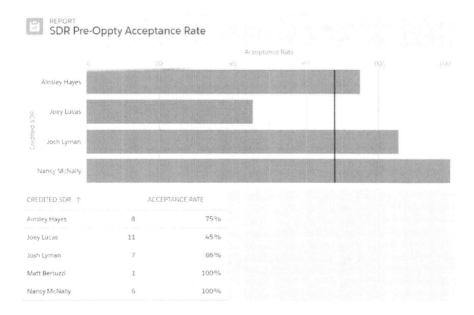

REPORT
SDR Pre-Oppty Acceptance Rate

CREDITED SDR ↑		ACCEPTANCE RATE
Ainsley Hayes	8	75%
Joey Lucas	11	45%
Josh Lyman	7	86%
Matt Bertuzzi	1	100%
Nancy McNally	6	100%

Figure 20.4 – Pre-Opportunity acceptance rate report

This should give SDR leadership a good view into acceptance and rejection. From this report, you'll immediately notice that three of four reps are above the target line for acceptance rate. Is "Joey Lucas" passing poorly-qualified meetings that don't meet the criteria? Or is it just bad luck and random noise? These are important questions and this type of reporting can alert managers to dig deeper.

The SDRs themselves will likely have different questions. Namely, where do all the meetings I've passed current stand? You should consider using a bucket field to collapse many *Opportunity* **Stages** into fewer "buckets" as shown in figure 20.5:

STAGE	Bucket
Closed No Oppty	Rejected
Closed Lost	Lost
SDR-Sourced	Pending
Stages 1-n	Accepted
Closed Won	Won

Figure 20.5 – Collapsing stages into buckets

Without the bucket field, each *Opportunity* stage becomes its own row. It can be difficult for an SDR to quickly get a sense of where the pipeline they've sourced stands. An SDR's "My Opptys Created QTD" report might look like the figure 20.6 below. With this report, an SDR can orient quickly to where their deals sit and the impact they've had.

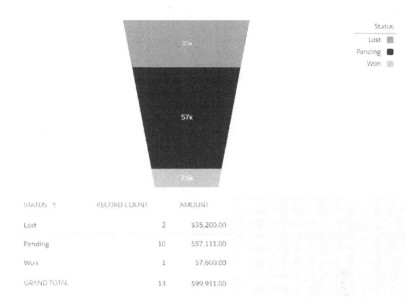

STATUS ↑	RECORD COUNT	AMOUNT
Lost	2	$35,200.00
Pending	10	$57,111.00
Won	1	$7,600.00
GRAND TOTAL	13	$99,911.00

Figure 20.6 – Status bucket reporting

You also might compare acceptance rates across account executives. There will be natural variation. But with formal qualification criteria, and the benefits of passing meetings round-robin, acceptance rates shouldn't vary too widely. In the example below (figure 20.7), Charlie and CJ are within a reasonable range. But Matt Santos isn't. Is Matt using overly strict criteria? Or is he truly receiving lower quality meetings? That's something you'll want to spot early and dig into more deeply

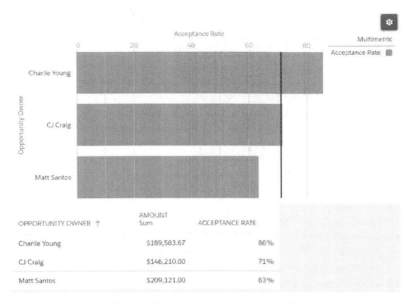

OPPORTUNITY OWNER ↑	AMOUNT Sum	ACCEPTANCE RATE
Charlie Young	$189,583.67	86%
CJ Craig	$146,210.00	71%
Matt Santos	$209,121.00	63%

Figure 20.7 – Acceptance rate by AE

At this point, I hope you're convinced of the merits of the "Stage 0: Pre-Opportunity" approach. It makes it easy for SDRs to book appointments and "pass" a uniform and sufficiently-detailed summary of the meeting. Account executives are given a Salesforce record to accept or reject—and aren't taken too far outside their normal *Opportunity* workflow. And finally, reporting is rock solid back to lead source and campaign, up to individual SDR/AE results, and down to pipeline and revenue impact.

PART 5

REPORT

Ninety percent of all drivers think they are above average behind the wheel.

—DR. RICHARD THALER

143

CHAPTER 21

⚡

LOOK WHERE THE HOLES AREN'T

THROUGHOUT THE FIRST FOUR PARTS OF THIS BOOK, we touched on reporting several times. In this fifth and final part, we'll delve much deeper. But first, a story.

Abraham Wald was a mathematician born in 1902 in what was then Austria–Hungary. In the late 1930s, after the Nazis conquered Austria, Wald left Europe for the United States. During the Second World War, he worked as part of the Statistical Research Group (SRG) at Columbia University. You can think of the SRG as the mathematical research equivalent of the Manhattan project. During the course of the war, the Center for Naval Analyses turned to the SRG for help.

American planes, returning from campaigns over Europe, were covered in bullet holes. As you might expect, these holes were found in many places on returning aircraft. This posed a problem. The military needed to determine where to add additional armor—so that bombers could take damage and still return home safely. But armor is heavy and they also needed to reduce airplane weight to gain more distance. So they turned to Abraham Wald and the SRG.

One solution was to add armor to the parts of the planes that had the most bullets holes. Returning planes were found to have fewer holes (per square foot) on their engines than on their fuselages, fuel systems, wings, rudders, and so on. Most people would react that common-sense says that the areas hit most frequently need additional protection. But Abraham Wald was no common man.

Wald deduced that bombers taking fire in their engines were less likely to make it back. His insight was that armor needed to be placed where the bullet holes *weren't* found—namely the engines.

This is one of those insights that is immediately apparent after the solution is revealed. As legend has it, the military acted on the recommendations and untold numbers of bombers returned from missions thanks to Wald and the power of counterintuitive thinking.

I'm sharing this story for two reasons. One, it's an awesome anecdote. Feel free to steal it and enthrall your friends and coworkers. Two, the majority of sales development reporting is focused on "where the bullet holes are." On job descriptions, companies may be seeking "individuals who can use analytics to generate critical business insights," but in reality, too often they task them with building reports of the same input and output metrics again and again. The best reporting, the kind that inspires action and changes the trajectory of group performance, never forgets *to look where the holes aren't*. And that's our goal for the remainder of this book.

I've divided the following chapters by audience and ask—whom the reporting is built to inform and what decisions they're looking to make with it:

- ▶ **Marketing**- What's happening with the demand we're creating? What's our impact on pipeline and revenue?

- ▶ **Individual SDRs** - How am I doing? Where do I rank? What should I be doing next?

- ▶ **SDR managers**- In aggregate, how is the group performing? Which reps are struggling? Where should I direct my coaching?

- ▶ **Senior leadership**- What's the impact on the business? Where are we trending?

First, a few quick disclaimers. One, *I'm going to avoid acronym speak*. The terms *Inquiry, MQL, SAL,* and *SQL* are used regularly in our universe. But the problem is that not every company uses the same order. For Company A, the waterfall flows: *Marketing Qualified Lead -> Sales Accepted Lead -> Sales Qualified Lead*. But for another, the order runs: *Marketing Qualified Lead -> Sales Qualified Lead -> Sales Accepted Lead*.

That makes life a tad difficult.

As I have done throughout this book, I'll stick to the language used in figure 21.1 below. That should keep things nice and clean.

Figure 21.1 – Waterfall flow guide

Disclaimer number two. *Reports are for informing decisions.* Period. Too much sales operations and SDR leadership time is consumed building reports that provide data, but don't give birth to action. I'm sure you'll find that I missed a few of your favorite reports. That's a good thing. I'm trying to stick to the core of SDR reporting. To borrow a line from *Hamlet,* "There are more things in heaven and earth, Horatio, than are dreamt of in your philosophy." Said another way, there's almost no limit to how many ways you can report on SDR data within Salesforce. But running reports that aren't acted upon makes about as much sense as cooking an elaborate holiday meal and then going out for Chinese food.

The risk is going a mile wide on informing and never more than an inch deep on action. Reporting is a large portion of the *what* behind sales operations. But it isn't the *why.* Sales operations exists to help reps, managers, executives, and companies make better decisions. To do that, we need to reel in our users and ground them in *actionable reporting* not just *interesting data.*

Disclaimer number three. *I have a bias for absolute values.* There is an intense devotion to ratios in sales development reporting. They can be extremely important—recall our "Connect Rate by Hour" and "Win Rate Matrix" reports. But they can also focus on the forest and miss the trees. Think of it this way. Say you have six houseplants and you kill five. You buy six more and only four die this time. From a ratio perspective, you've improved 100%. Amazing! In reality, you're still a pretty lousy gardener. Or consider a high connect rate and a meeting acceptance rate, for example. Those can be great indicators. But if the total number of dials and total amount of SDR-sourced pipeline are way behind quotas, do they really matter?

It may seem like I'm harping on this point, but it's only because I've seen too many sales operation and SDR leaders crashed upon the rocky shores of ratio reporting. Ratios are like GPS, they are fantastic tools for knowing where you are, where you've been, and where you're going. But they aren't a replacement for looking out your windshield. They won't do a thing to help you avoid the huge dump truck that just backed out and is blocking your lane.

When in doubt, I prefer to compare a result metric to a goal. Optimizing rates and ratios are important for groups in the post-scale stage. For the rest of us, it's better to report results that are meaningful to the business than to focus on elegant and over-precise ratios. I mean no disrespect to great industry benchmark data providers. They do interesting and (sometimes) important work. But you can beat every benchmark conversion rate you find on-line and still get fired. *How rude!* They are certainly directionally helpful, but don't let them distract you from your real goals.

One more quality conversation, one more meeting, one more accepted opportunity, one more win. Those results are "buy them a beer" worthy. One percentage point improvement, on the other hand, does little to wow senior leadership.

Okay, enough disclaimers. Time to dig in.

CHAPTER 22

⚡

TIMESTAMP EVERYTHING

KNOWING WHEN A RECORD WAS CREATED, reached a status, or crossed a threshold is one of the most useful tools for sales development reporting. As we've covered earlier, there are many stages in the prospect-to-win process. It is hard to report on that entire lifecycle without timestamp data. In case you aren't familiar, timestamping is commonly used to fill in a hidden date field when a record reaches a milestone or crosses a threshold. Common examples include:

▶ When marketing passes an "MQL" prospect to a sales development rep

▶ When the first attempt is made on that "MQL"

▶ When a meeting is set as a "Stage 0: Pre-Opportunity"

▶ And so on . . .

With timestamping, you can report on conversion rates (i.e. how many "MQLs" become "Stage 0: Pre-Opportunity") or duration (i.e. what's the velocity from "Stage 0: Pre-Opportunity" to "Closed Won" in days). Jordy Brazier is Senior Director of Sales Operations at Qubole. I asked him for his philosophy on timestamping. "Full tracking of the prospect-to-win lifecycle isn't possible without time stamps. There is huge value in reporting on the history of a single lead or groups of leads. How many days until the MQLs are picked up by an SDR? How long from accepted opportunities to wins? And so on. This gives you full A-Z visibility, not only duration but the fall-off between stages."

What Jordy outlined is the beauty and the promise of full visibility. Assuming you're using *Contact, Accounts,* and *Opportunities*, here's how you
might use timestamps:

TIMESTAMP WHEN	OBJECT
Set to "MQL"	Contact
Set to "Working" or "Reached"	Contact
Set to "Qualified"	Contact
"SDR Pre-Opportunity" is created	Opportunity
AE accepts into pipeline	Opportunity
SDR-Sourced Opportunity is "Closed Won"	Opportunity

Figure 22.1 - Timestamps

Unfortunately, there's a wrinkle: the fact that this A-Z process involves
multiple objects. You can easily report, as Jordy suggests, on duration and
fall-off between stages on a single object. But reporting across objects—what
percentage of "reach prospects" from last quarter were "Closed Won" for instance—isn't easily done.

You have a few options. One, you can use automation to sync date fields
between objects. Visual Workflow is one way to traverse Contact Roles and
update the *Contact* object when an *Opportunity* changes. Option two, use a
3rd party tool. Full Circle Insights is an amazing, paid app on the Appexchange
which elegantly solves this issue. Option three, just deal with it. You can't get
every waterfall metric into a single report, funnel chart, or dashboard component. But you can get the metrics, from different reports, onto a single
dashboard. That's good enough for me. Until your scale and complexity de-
mands a different approach, it's probably good enough for you too.

The mechanics of timestamping are quite simple. Back in the Bronze Age,
we Salesforce admins would use a series of workflow rules to populate custom
date fields. Change the **Lead Status** from "MQL" to "Working"? Boom, time
stamp! So on and so forth. Today, I prefer to use Process Builder to consoli-
date many workflow rules into fewer processes. You'll have one on *Contacts*
and one on *Opportunities*. (Note: if your reps are using *Leads,* there's a third.)

Before building the automation, you'll want to create two custom fields for each timestamp. A date field will catch the date of the stage change and a formula checkbox field will return unchecked (FALSE) when the corresponding date field is blank. You'll use the former to calculate days between stages and the latter for absolute values and ratios. For a formula, you can use something like:

```
NOT(
    ISBLANK( YourDateField__c )
)
```

If Your Date field is blank—ISBLANK equals TRUE—then return the opposite: FALSE. And vice versa. Putting it all together, you can create a "Sales Operations" section on the *Contact* and *Opportunity* page layouts (figure 22.2 below):

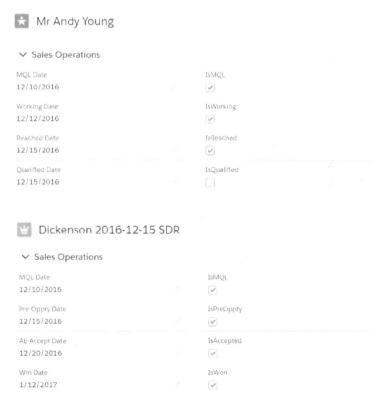

Figure 22.2 – Sales operations sections

Now I know you might object to creating extra fields when **Created Date** and **Close Date** do the same thing. But I'm a bit fanatical about field naming. I prefer these fields are named similarly and presented in their own section. I find it makes things easy for leaders to decipher reporting and read a record's "history." But to each his or her own.

Now that you have the date and checkbox fields, you have everything you'll need to begin funnel / lifecycle reporting. And that's exactly what we'll cover in the following chapter.

CHAPTER 23

⚡

MEASURE MARKETING IMPACT

IN THE FANTASTIC BOOK *Cracking the Sales Management Code*, Jason Jordan and Michelle Vazzana identified 306 metrics that leaders use to manage their teams. They grouped all the metrics into three categories:

▶ **RESULTS:** the outcomes that are incredibly important to the business but outside the control of sales management and reps

▶ **OBJECTIVES:** areas that can be influenced but still are outside the reps' direct control

▶ **ACTIVITIES:** things that are under the direct control of the reps and can be proactively managed

Whenever I think about reporting, I like to keep these three buckets in mind. *Results* are important, but leaders can't directly manage (and reps can't directly control) them. It's important that we peel back the onion and highlight the underlying *objective* and *activity* metrics. As we discussed in the previous chapter, there's no easy way to show a prospect's full lifecycle in one report or chart. But by breaking your reports in half—"MQL to Pre-Opportunity" on the one and "Pre-Opportunity to Win" on the other—you can still do some amazing things.

Let's focus on marketing. Nearly every marketing group supplies their SDR team with prospects to convert into meetings. Considering results from last month, the headline metrics they care about might include:

► **RESULTS-** number of MQLs delivered, number of resulting meetings, total pipeline sourced by marketing

► **OBJECTIVES-** Disqualification rate, MQL-to-meeting rate, recycle reasons, and so on

► **ACTIVITIES-** attempts per MQL, MQL-to-working rate

Leaving aside Campaign and Campaign influence reporting, there are quite a number of components above. These can be combined into a very informative "Marketing | SDR" dashboard. Your dashboard might look like figure 23.1 below:

Figure 23.1 - "Marketing | SDR" dashboard

Reading this dashboard tell us that 93 "MQLs" were generated for this given campaign—below the target of 100. And that 12 "Pre-Opportunity" meetings were booked—exceeding the target of 10 (and with 15 prospects still being worked). Those 12 "Pre-Opportunity" meetings account for $61K in pipeline with 3 wins already on the books. Additionally, marketing can see the distribution of **Recycle Reasons** (overwhelmingly "No contact") as well as "Rejection Rate" (roughly 4%). You might add or remove components, but this should give you a good starting point to examine the results of an inbound SDR team.

Or say that marketing is concerned with the speed of "MQL" response. Perhaps an initiative has been underway to increase the percentage of "MQLs" with a first attempt on the day they're assigned. Since you're already tracking **MQL Date** and **Working Date**, this is an easy task. You can create two more custom formula fields as follows:

FIELD NAME	TYPE	FORMULA
Days to Attempt	Formula (Numeric)	Working_Date__c - MQL_Date__c
Attempted Same Day	Formula (Checkbox)	MQL_Date__c = Working_Date__c

Figure 23.2 – Custom formulas for days

With these two fields, your report might resemble figure 23.3 below. Note: since "MQLs" will often become *sales-ready* on weekends and holidays, getting to 0.0 average **Days to Attempt** isn't a reasonable goal.

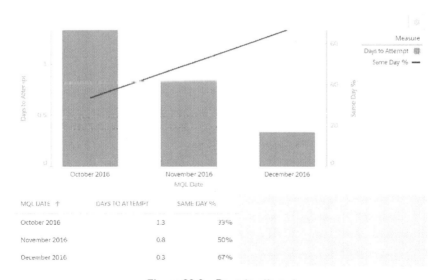

MQL DATE ↑	DAYS TO ATTEMPT	SAME DAY %
October 2016	1.3	33%
November 2016	0.8	50%
December 2016	0.3	67%

Figure 23.3 – Days to attempt

From this report, marketing can see that the focus on shrinking response time has been effective. From October to December, the average **Days to Attempt** fell by 77%—from 1.3 to 0.3 days. And the percentage of "MQLs" attempted the day they were assigned more than doubled.

Know Your Funnel

I've yet to meet the marketing team that when asked "would you like to be able to report on funnel volume, conversion, and duration?" replied with anything other than an enthusiastic *hell yes!* Comparing campaigns as they progress through the funnel is hugely valuable. Say your marketing team came to you with questions about results from a recent industry tradeshow. They might ask:

▶ How many of the MQLs did we reach?

▶ How many became meetings?

▶ How many opportunities and how much pipeline did we source?

▶ What was the velocity (speed in days) from MQL to meeting? And from meeting to win?

Now that you've built checkbox and date timestamps, you can accomplish just that. For the "Big Tradeshow" in question, figures 23.4 and 23.5 show a 14% "MQL" to "Pre-Opportunity" conversion rate. And a 22% conversion from "Pre-Opportunity" to "Win."

CAMPAIGN ↑	WORKING-REACHED	REACH-QUALIFIED	MQL-PREOPPTY
Big Tradeshow	43%	33%	14%

Figure 23.4 - "MQL" to "Pre-Opportunity"

REPORT
PreOppty-Win

CAMPAIGN ↑	PREOPPTY-ACCEPTED	ACCEPTED-WIN	PREOPPTY-WIN
Big Tradeshow	68%	32%	22%

Figure 23.5 - "Pre-Opportunity" to "Win"

From there, reporting on number of "Pre-Opportunities" and pipeline sourced is easy. Getting the velocity in days, requires a bit more work. On the *Opportunity* side of the house, you can use native reporting to get to "Stage Duration." But that doesn't really work for *Contact* and *Leads*. Earlier, you defined a set of date fields to hold the date entered for key milestones. Now, you can add a set of duration formula fields that show the number of days between each.

The beauty of this solution is its flexibility. You can calculate **Days to Reached** duration, **Days to Qualified** duration, and separately **Days MQL to Pre-Oppty** (figure 23.6 below). With the addition of these duration fields, you can deliver the velocity data that marketing needs to make informed decisions.

REPORT
Days to PreOppty

CAMPAIGN ↑	DAYS TO ATTEMPT Avg	DAYS TO REACHED Avg	DAYS TO QUALIFIED Avg	DAYS MQL TO PREOPPTY Avg
Big Tradeshow	1	7	4	12

Figure 23.6 - Days MQL to Pre-Oppty

Let's return to one of the disclaimers at the start of this part of the book. *Reports are for informing decisions, not satisfying curiosity.* It's easy enough to build fantastic reporting, like those above, for your marketing group. You might share them and even be greeted by, "Wow! These are great. Thank you!" But if you were to follow up and no action was taken, you've spun your wheels and the business is no better off.

For the big tradeshow example above, perhaps the "MQL-to-PreOppty" rate was half those of normal prospects. But the "PreOppty-to-Win" rates were sky high. What should marketing do with this information? Should they invest in this tradeshow again next year? How should the SDR and AE processes be adjusted to improve these results? These are questions that lead to action—and not just data for data's sake.

Build with the Future in Mind

I ran across an idea on the Salesforce Success Community the other day. The poster wrote:

> *"It would be useful to be able to filter by Created By: Role in Reports. For example, our Inside Sales Team is responsible for creating Opportunities, which they will eventually transfer to the appropriate Field Sales person. We would like to be able to filter by Created By: Role. 'Created By' works when you have a small number of individuals to filter, but it is not scalable."*

I couldn't agree more with that final sentence.

When you have three SDRs, filtering reports by **Created By: Full Name** is easy enough. But when you have ten or more—with new SDRs joining and senior reps being promoted—you won't want to edit each underlying report over and over again. I brought this up with consultant and fellow Salesforce MVP Lauren Jordan. She suggested leveraging the **Created By: Role** and **Created By: Manager** fields. "I've worked with companies in the past that put a strong focus on marketing operations and measurement. They wanted total clarity into pipeline contribution. Looking at all opportunities, what are the inbound SDRs bringing in? How does that compare to the outbound SDRs? And then breaking it down by manager, what are each teams' results? You have to build upfront to be able to report on these down the road."

You might consider creating a custom report type to achieve Lauren's vision. The standard "Opportunity" report type lacks the **Created By: Role** and **Created By: Manager** fields. You can simply create a new report type and make sure to include those fields under "Fields Available for Reports."

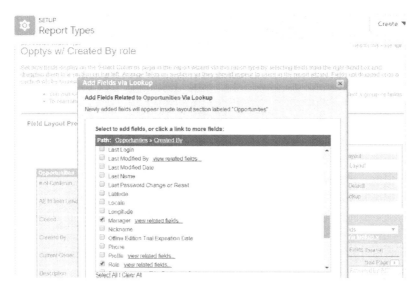

Figure 23.7 – New report type for role and manager fields

Or you could create custom fields on the *Opportunity* object: **CreatedBy's Role** and **CreatedBy's Manager**. You should use automation to populate these fields. Creating a custom formula field (that spans to the *User* object) works well enough. But it falls apart when reps are promoted or switch teams. Imagine you have an inbound SDR that is promoted to an outbound role. Or say an outbound SDR advances to an account executive position. What do you do with their *User* record? Logically, you would update the **Role** and the **Manager**. Seems easy enough. But if your *Opportunity* formula fields reference those *User records*, you've got a problem. Your historical **Created By: Role** and **Created By: Manager** reports are incorrect. Not good.

If you have a high-rate of promotion and team transfers, you need a strategy to preserve "year to date" and "year over year" reporting. Using automation to populate a static **CreatedBy's Role** and **CreatedBy's Manager** is any easy way to do just that.

CHAPTER 24

SURFACE SDR METRICS

I ASKED LIZ CAIN from OpenView Venture Partners for her philosophy on which metrics to share with the SDRs themselves. We met Liz back in Part 3 where she shared her advice on allowing reps to work from list views. "Fundamentally there are two different types of dashboards appropriate for SDRs: *working* and *output*. Both are important, but serve different ends. The working dashboard answers 'what am I supposed to do today, this week, or this month?' This includes new leads, overdue tasks, and so on. The results dashboard answers 'how am I doing against my goals?' It can include activities, meetings versus goal, and pipeline impact—number of accepted opportunities and amount of pipeline sourced."

Liz gives us a lot to digest there. I love her concept of separating *working* and *results* dashboards. Too often these types of metrics are crammed into a single, eye-chart dashboard. Or broken into dozens and dozens of individual reports. By limiting the number of places a rep has to go to learn something—and focusing on the specific questions they're looking to have answered—you can create truly useful Salesforce analytics. Let's start with the working dashboard. To my mind, the key answers to "what am I supposed to do today?" include:

- How many new "MQLs" have I been assigned?
- How many prospects are due today? How many are overdue?
- How many meetings are scheduled for today and tomorrow?
- What is the status of those meetings?

You can certainly create this *working dashboard* as a traditional Salesforce dashboard. Or you might create a custom Lightning home page. You can take the four items listed above and create an underlying report (with charts) for each. Then add "Report Chart" components to the Lightning home page for your sales development reps. This brings the dashboard experience directly to the reps on log in.

You might also add a rich text area with a favorite quote and links to other key information on the sidebar (see figure 24.1 below).

Figure 24.1 – Customized Lightning home page

The second type of dashboards focus on *results*. If every SDR had the mindset that they were running their own business—they're the CEO of setting meetings for account executive clients—which indicators would they want to stay on top of? Likely the list would include:

► **RESULTS-** meetings set, meetings accepted, $ pipeline sourced

► **OBJECTIVES-** *MQL to Pre-Oppty* and *Pre-Oppty to Accepted* rates

► **TRENDING-** what's the direction of my meeting setting business

Preston Clark serves as president of the education tech company EverFi. We discussed how he keeps his team focused on the metrics that matter. "I'm mindful to avoid getting so absorbed in the complexity that we lose sight of our bigger goals. When I pass by an SDR who's grabbing a coffee in the kitchen, I'll ask, 'How much pipeline did you help source this week? How many demos did your team complete?' I expect him or her to know those metrics at all times. Yes, SDRs have to work on their number of dials, call to connect ratios, email open rates, etc. But they need to obsess over the outputs that drive the business forward. It's easy to lose track of those amidst the sea of other metrics."

I couldn't agree more. The tendency with sales development is to optimize the "small ball" stuff—template performance, optimal number of emails, and so on—but the risk is in losing sight of the *do or die* metrics Preston laid out.

To focus your SDRs, you can combine these metrics into a personal "My Results MTD" dashboard (see figure 24.2). If I were an SDR and wanted to know "how my business is doing" that dashboard would suit me just fine. How about you?

Figure 24.2 – "My Results MTD" Dashboard

Build a Team Leaderboard

In addition to these *working* and *results* dashboards, most companies use leaderboards with their SDR teams. I discussed leaderboard design with Megan Pietruszka, Sales Operations at LevelUp. "In our rep facing leaderboard, we don't present conversion rates and trending metrics," she shared. "We include what the SDRs care about most: who set the most meetings this month, who has sourced the most pipeline dollars, how are we tracking against our team goal, and so on. Our reps can always access this dashboard, but we also schedule it to go out to them weekly."

I'm a big fan of Megan's approach to choosing metrics. In their "My Results MTD" dashboard, your reps can see all the KPIs associated with their performance. It's a mistake to take those same metrics, stack rank reps against each other, and call that a leaderboard. It's important to choose *activity* and *outcome* metrics alongside your *results*. A dashboard that highlights only meetings passed might feature the same winners (hall of fame) and losers (wall of shame) month after month. Rather than encouraging healthy competition, this can become a major demotivator. "Kyle and Trish are at the top again. Surprise, surprise." By including activity and outcome metrics, you are changing the terms of the competition. It isn't just about the destination, but about the journey it takes to get there.

Think of it this way. In order to generate "SDR-sourced opportunities" reps need to book "pre-opportunity" meetings. To book meetings, reps need to have "Next Step" conversations. To have those quality conversations, reps need to make live connects. And in order to have live connects, they need to execute outbound activity. Many of those components are either directly (working harder) or indirectly (working smarter) under rep control. Your "SDR Weekly Leaderboard" might resemble figure 24.3 below.

Figure 24.3 – Leaderboard

This type of leaderboard gives reps multiple opportunities to take first place. As you can see, Nancy McNally has taken first place in the *result* metrics of "Meetings" and "Pipeline Dollars." But Ainsley Hayes and Josh Lyman each placed first in another *outcome* and *activity* category.

One other approach you might consider layering in is a "daily huddle report" (DHR).

Chris Corcoran, cofounder and Managing Partner of memoryBlue, shared this "DHR" concept with me. "Each morning, the SDRs, managers, and senior leaders all receive an email with key results for the prior day as well as month-to-date. Each manager holds a daily standup with his or her team to review the metrics and provide color. My cofounder Marc holds a separate daily huddle with all the managers to do the same. We think of the DHR like the sports page for our company—reviewing stats, sharing successes, and checking the standings."

Note: as of this writing, scheduling dashboards haven't been brought to the Lightning Experience. They're listed under the "Future" category on the Lightning Experience Roadmap (which can be found at https://help.salesforce.com/articleView?id=lex_roadmap.htm). Until then, screenshots and manual emails are one workaround. Another is to build your "DHR report" as a dashboard in Classic and take advantage of daily scheduled refreshes—even though the results will appear in the Classic formatting.

Schedule Reports the Right Way

I want to end this chapter by discussing the concept (and many missteps) of using scheduled reports. In case you aren't familiar, scheduling reports allows a report to "run itself" on a schedule and send email results to the users you specify. Scheduled reports are a fantastic way to *prompt* reps and leaders to do something. But just as in Stan Lee's *Spiderman* universe, with great power comes great responsibility. Here are some rules of thumb for using scheduled reports:

► **When you want reps to take action *right now*, use a mid-day scheduled report.** Too often, I see reps being emailed activity reports at the end of the day to "encourage" higher activity levels. But at the end of the day, it's too late. And by tomorrow, all will have been forgotten.

► **When you want reps and leaders to recap and reflect, use a Friday afternoon scheduled.** This works really well to prompt a retrospective conversation. What went well this week? Where did I get off track? How can I prevent that next week? And so on.

► **When you want to publicize the Hall of Fame, use a monthly scheduled report.** Reps and first-line managers are already plugged into their key results dashboards. They don't need the email reminder. But if you're going upstream to senior leaders, don't expect them to log in and find the team dashboard or report. A monthly schedule report or dashboard is a good way to publicize the group's success with executive leadership.

CHAPTER 25

⚡

SUPPORT LEADERSHIP WITH DATA

IN WRITING THIS BOOK, I interviewed a baker's dozen of first-line SDR leaders. I asked each of them, "In your results dashboard, what are the KPIs you care about?" It became a bit of a running joke as they'd invariably reply, "I'm sure you're hearing the same exact thing, but I measure activities, conversations, meetings passed, meetings accepted, and trending." The tribal wisdom of sales development leaders suggests two core types of reporting. The first focuses on results and rates. The second analyzes trending over time.

A *results and rates* dashboard provides leadership with the key metrics to monitor group performance. In figure 25.1 below, you can several rate metrics that are helpful to make comparisons between SDRs. You are trying to draw the manager's eye to problems. In the "rates" section, the manager can quickly note when a rep significantly leads or lags their peers.

METRIC	MEASURES
Connect Rate	Is the rep receiving quality leads and making outreach at optimal times?
Reach Rate	Is the rep effectively executing the cadence to maximize MQL-to-Reach rate?
Meeting Rate	Is the rep opening, closing, and positioning the meeting effectively when they do reach a prospect?

Figure 25.1 - My team's results

Doug Landis is VP of Sales Productivity at Box. In a session at HubSpot's *Inbound Sales Day*, he shared, "A lot of people think of coaching as asking

167

what went well? What do you think you missed? The reality in many cases is that coaching needs to be a bit more directive. Here's what you're doing well. Here's what you're not doing well. And here's where you need to improve. To make for better coaching conversations, managers need to be empowered with their 'sales equation.' Knowing that you're x number of deals away from quota is one piece of that. But how do reps know what they need to do in order to get to their number? How do they know how they're performing compared to peers or compared to company benchmarks? The idea of the sales equation is to define the key dials that managers should be tracking and share them with the reps themselves."

Let's take a look at a team dashboard to compare peers as Doug suggests. In figure 25.2 below, you might spot that Josh Lyman is underperforming his peers by 20% with only seven meetings passed. His total activity levels, connect rate, and reach rate are where they should be. But his meeting rate is well below his peers.

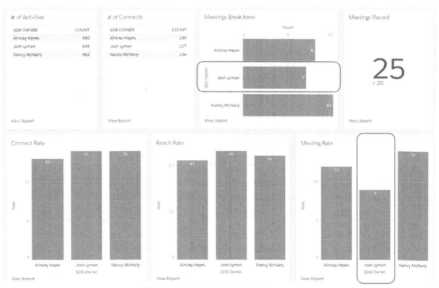

Figure 25.2 - Team dashboard

Josh's manager might double-jack in and listen to live calls or rely on call recording software to get a sense for what Josh is doing on live connects. *Is he falling flat with opening statements? Are basic objections shutting him down? Or is he giving up at the slightest pushback and failing at challenging prospects?* And so on

Looking at an "Average Days" report (figure 25.3 below), it's clear that Josh's average duration between "Reached" and "Qualified" is much longer than his peers'. *Is it a closing issue? Is he failing to effectively overcome objections?*

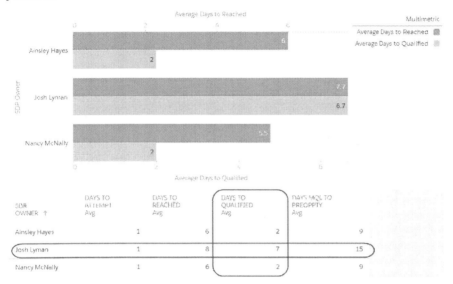

Figure 25.3 - "Average Days" report

Neither report nor dashboard can diagnose a specific gap in sales skills. But they can point managers in the correct direction. Dashboards and reports, like those shared above, can serve as a first step for breaking down the "sales equation," diagnosing the issue, and having metrics-informed coaching conversations.

Take Action with Trends

The second manager-level reporting you should consider focuses on *trending over time.* Anthony Zhang, VP of Sales and Marketing at CoCounselor, shared, "Trending is something I pay a lot of attention to. If inbound leads are down this month, what does that mean for next month? If meetings are way up this month, is that a momentary fluke or are we steadily improving over time? By looking at the trends, I can spot the leading indicators and make adjustments."

Say, for example, you knew that the number of new "MQLs" was directly correlated with meetings passed. It's likely that, month-to-month, the number of new prospects bounces a fair bit. How do you report on the trend? If you're like me, you weren't born with a preternatural gift for calculating moving averages in your head. Thankfully, we can make use of the Salesforce formula function called *PREVGROUPVAL*. Sounds tantalizing, no?

Salesforce documents the PREVGROUPVAL function as "calculating values relative to a peer grouping. If there's no previous grouping, the function returns a null value." For our purposes, PREVGROUPVAL gives us a 3-month moving average of results, by taking the average of *this month and the two months prior*.

Returning to our new "MQLs" report, your results might resemble figure 25.4 below:

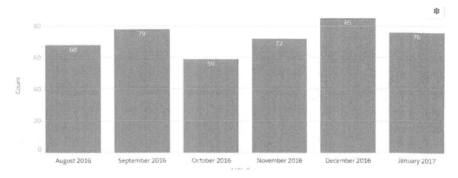

Figure 25.4 – "MQLs" report by month

With the naked eye, it's hard to spot the trend there. Give it a shot. Do you think we're down, flat, or up? Okay, time for the big reveal. The trend is . . . up. See the darker line in figure 25.5 below for the 3-month moving average. The 3-month moving average is up to 77.7 in January from 72.0 in December.

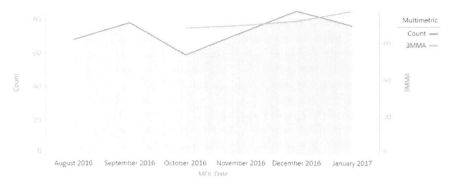

Figure 25.5 – Moving average report

To build this report, you can add a "3MMA" custom summary field with the syntax below. The formula adds the current month, the month prior, and the month before that and then divides the total by three to return the moving average.

```
(Lead.Number__c:SUM + PREVGROUPVAL(Lead.Number__c:SUM,
Lead.MQL_Date__c) + PREVGROUPVAL(Lead.Number__c:SUM,
Lead.MQL_Date__c, 2)) / 3
```

There's one more trend trick that you should have in your back pocket. Namely, *reporting on change in trend*. I had a VP of Sales Development push me to the edge of my Salesforce reporting limits—and back to college math class—to deliver this one. Your change in trend reporting answers the following: *by what percentage is the current moving average up or down from the prior?* At first blush, this might seem like a theoretically interesting and practically useless question. But there's real power in this metric.

Monthly values are jumpy. Peaks and valleys are natural. Three-month moving averages can smooth those out, but it takes time for a new trend to emerge. The *change in trend* can surface the early stages of a change much more quickly.

Returning once again to our new "MQLs" reporting, we knew that the 3-month moving average was steadily increasing. But with your *change in trend* reporting, in figure 25.6 below you can see that the rate of that increase is accelerating.

171

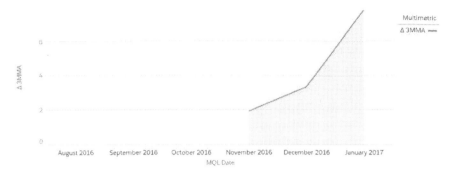

Figure 25.6 – Change in trend report

Your formula for this custom summary field should resemble:

```
((Lead.Number__c:SUM + PREVGROUPVAL(Lead.Number__c:SUM,
Lead.MQL_Date__c) + PREVGROUPVAL(Lead.Number__c:SUM,
Lead.MQL_Date__c, 2)) / 3)
/
((PREVGROUPVAL(Lead.Number__c:SUM, Lead.MQL_Date__c) +
PREVGROUPVAL(Lead.Number__c:SUM, Lead.MQL_Date__c, 2) +
PREVGROUPVAL(Lead.Number__c:SUM, Lead.MQL_Date__c, 3)) / 3)
- 1
```

It calculates the change in moving average by taking *this month and the two months prior* and comparing it to *two, three, and four months ago* (e.g., November-January compared to October-December).

These reports are particularly helpful as an early warning system. For example, if your new "MQL" volume drops for two months in a row, how significant is the change? For the VP of Sales Development who wanted these reports, 5% was her threshold. Anytime the moving average for her key metrics dropped by 5%+, red lights started flashing and alarms started blaring.

CHAPTER 26

⚡

DELIVER "DO OR DIE" DATA

"AS A TEENAGER, I was a valet at a luxury hotel in Los Angeles," shared Preston Clark, the president at EverFi who earlier shared his view on metrics that drive the business forward. "I learned to reverse park Ferraris and 700-series BMWs. The hardest part of the job was reversing into tight spots during rush periods—without scratching the cars. We had this mantra to 'always trust your mirrors' when reversing. It was hard at first because your tendency is to doubt your mirrors–you want to get out and double check before you risk scratching a $250k car. But there wasn't time for that."

"I think of sales development the same way. There's a lot of activity metrics that go into a successful SDR machine, but I have to know there are two or three 'mirrors' that I can trust unequivocally. You'll meet a lot of CEOs and founders who have a hard time trusting SDR metrics. I get it. 'Look, we scheduled 20 demos this week!' What's a CEO supposed to do with that metric? As leaders, it's important that we elevate the key metrics or 'mirrors' that we need everyone to trust. Add too many key metrics, and it starts to feel like we don't know how to get where we're going. The minutiae matters to the finely tuned machine you're building, but make sure those above and below you are always anchored to the key metrics that drive the business."

I absolutely love this story.

"Trusting your mirrors" is a phrase I've repeated many times since my conversation with Preston. And I hope it resonates with you, too. Building SDR reports for the executive team is about delivering the *do or die* data and focusing on impact to the business. As a starting point, your "SDR Impact this Quarter" dashboard might include:

▶ Number, percentage, and $ value of SDR-sourced *Opportunities*

▶ Leaderboard of top three SDRs

▶ Pipeline breakdown (won, lost, and open)

▶ Pipeline growth over time

Figure 26.1 – "Do or die" data reporting

This should give your executive team a solid feel for sales development's impact to the business as well as the general direction of results—down, flat, or up. One piece that won't likely be asked for, but you should include anyway, is a "top x number of SDRs" component. Your reps have a tough job and the fact that senior leadership knows the names of (at least a few) team members can be hugely motivating.

The "SDR Impact this Quarter" dashboard answers the question, *how is this team affecting the business?* Your executive team likely also cares about a separate question, *how do these opportunities compare to non-SDR-*

sourced ones?

Compare Across Channels

For many companies, the growth path follows a familiar story. Founders are the first sales reps. Once product market fit is confirmed, accounts executives are hired. Shortly thereafter, marketing investments start to pay off. Significant demand is generated and an inbound SDR role is created. The company is firing on all cylinders and is on track to post a massive year. And then . . . next year's growth number is issued.

And it's a big stretch.

You can hire more account executives. But you can't reasonably increase quotas if reps are facing smaller territories. And what's more, the AEs lack the time (and inclination) to do much outbound prospecting. You can ask marketing to own a larger pipeline number. But that uplift only gets you part of the way there. So what's to be done? For many organizations, the answer is *outbound sales development.*

Patrick Purvis, DiscoverOrg's VP of Sales, shared a similar story with me. "When you're a sales leader with a number to hit, blaming marketing for a miss isn't an option. You own getting to the number. Outbound is something you spin up and see results immediately. In the last year, I scaled our SDR team from 5 reps to over 20. That engine has gone from generating under one-fifth to over half of our wins."

Newton's first law of motion applies to sales, too. *An object at rest stays at rest and an object in motion stays in motion.* Said another way, outbound prospecting takes more effort and intensity than qualifying inbound demand. Outbound deals generally have a longer sales cycle and lower win rate. To compensate for that, outbound groups go upmarket—targeting larger customers. Patrick shared that he closely monitors his outbound team's results to make sure they are doing just that.

Your starting *comparison metrics* might include:

▶ % of pipeline sourced (inbound SDRs, outbound SDRs, AEs)

▶ Sales cycles in days

▶ Average deal size

▶ Win rate

If your company can thrive exclusively off inbound marketing, color me impressed. To meet growth targets most companies need to go *allbound*, adding an outbound component to inbound. Figure 26.2 below above provides insight into results and an important check on assumptions. Generating pipeline from outbound activity is almost always going to be harder than converting inbound interest. These metrics will keep everyone on track and make sure you're targeting (and closing) opportunities that are "worthy" of outbound effort.

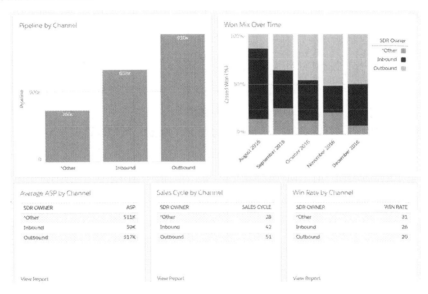

Figure 26.2 – Comparison metrics

PARTING THOUGHTS

⚡

THERE'S A NASA STORY you might have heard. It is popular enough to have become a meme. It goes:

When NASA first started sending up astronauts, they quickly discovered that ballpoint pens wouldn't work in zero gravity.

To combat the problem, NASA scientists spent a decade and $12 million to develop a pen that writes in zero gravity, upside down, on almost any surface including glass, and at temperatures ranging from below freezing to over 300 degrees Fahrenheit.

The Russians used a pencil.

The moral of this charming anecdote is that over-engineering is tempting and, without an effort towards thrift, waste and excess will run rampant. The real story is a bit more nuanced.

Space, it turns out, isn't like Earth. Pencil tips can break and will eventually need to be shaved. The resulting floating bits of debris are dangerous to astronauts and shuttles alike. Fisher Pen Company—a private business—developed an "anti-gravity" pen that uses pressurized nitrogen. You can buy it on Amazon right now for about $30.

From Gandalf, to Rory Gilmore, to perspectives from dozens of amazing executives, to a NASA fable. We've certainly tapped diverse sources of wisdom in this book.

I bring up this NASA story because too often "complex" is taken to mean "bad." The general sentiment seems to be: "Things are simpler in Salesforce Classic." "It's easier to use what we've built already." "I don't want to over-engineer, the users can just deal with workarounds." These arguments (or excuses) may be correct in the short term, but they miss a larger truth. Your users don't care how complex things are behind the scenes. They just want a pen that writes and won't break the shuttle. If this requires a lot of moving pieces, a bit of outside-the-box thinking, and a fair share of hacks, so be it.

I learned a lot writing these pages. And I hope, through reading them, you've learned, too. There's much I'm still discovering about the Lightning Experience. Lightning Console, Related List components, and the Utility Bar, for example, are areas I'm just beginning to explore. With each release, Lightning evolves and expands our options for delivering real value to our users.

One of the best parts of the Salesforce community is the Salesforce 'ohana (Hawaiian for family). With the #askforce hashtag on Twitter and the entire Success Community (https://success.salesforce.com), this 'ohana is always ready to lend support. I hope this won't be the end of our conversation. You can find me on Twitter (@mattbertuzzi) and active over on Success. *Lightning Now!* and *ButtonClick Admins* are two groups I spend a fair bit of time in as well.

If you picked up this book hoping to elevate your SDRs' experiences and/or to peek behind the curtain at Salesforce Lightning, I hope I've delivered on both counts. With Lightning and the growing wisdom of the entire sales operations community, we have the tools and the know-how to enable—perhaps even to delight—our reps.

If you've just entered the Salesforce ecosystem, congratulations! What a fantastic time and place to build your career. If you're a button-click admin veteran, I hope this book has inspired you and perhaps even reignited your passion for the platform.

What matters now, more than ever, is you.

No matter what your business card says, being a Salesforce admin means being a business analyst and change agent. Sit with your reps. Observe their daily workflow. Buy them a cup of coffee and let them gripe at you. Having a sales operations mindset means committing to improving user experience and designing subtle (yet powerful) automation.

Too many Salesforce implementations are laborious, lumbering, and limiting. Reps are weighed down by byzantine processes and time-consuming, click-heavy workstreams. Managers are drowning in reports, but lack the insights to lead their teams. Users and companies are crying out for someone to show them a better way.

The only question that remains is, "Will you answer the call?"

ACKNOWLEDGMENTS

⚡

You're the type of person who reads acknowledgments too? Cool!

I want to thank everyone who made this book a reality. I value every bit of input and help along the way.

Thank you to my brilliant wife, Kira, without whom this book would not have been possible. Special mention goes out to our two rescue dogs, Ranger and Cora, without whom this book would have been finished months earlier.

I am lucky to be a part of three amazing and supportive professional families. First to my work family, thank you. Trish Bertuzzi (hey ma!), Kyle Smith, and the entire Bridge Group team, your feedback was invaluable. Next to my sales and sales development family, I'll never be able to repay your generosity of time and insight. Finally, to my Salesforce family, thank you for your support. Much love, 'ohana.

Thank you to all the fantastic practitioners I interviewed for this book, listed here:

Alex Turner	Amyra Rand
Anthony Zhang	Ben Bronsther
Ben Sardella	Cathy Otocka
Chris Corcoran	Emma Lehman
Jay Schmidt	Jim McDonough
Jordy Brazier	Joy Shutters-Helbing
Kevin Dorsey	Kristi Guzman
Kristin Agnelli	Lauren Jordan
Liz Cain	Mallory Lee

Manny Alamwala	Megan Pietruszka
Melinda Smith	Morgan J. Ingram
Patrick Purvis	Pete Gracey
Phill Keene	Preston Clark
Rebecca Dente	Steve Richard
Vanessa Porter	Zoe Silverman

Special thank you to these members of the Salesforce community whom I learn from every day.

Amber Neill Boaz	Jared Miller
Beth Breisnes	Jeremiah Dohn
Christian Carter	Rebecca Dente
Gorav Seth	Steve Molis

INDEX

Made in the USA
Lexington, KY
08 November 2017